THE FALL OF
WESTERN MAN

MARK COLLETT
2017

Digital copies of *The Fall of Western Man* are **FREE** and are available for download at **www.thefallofwesternman.com**

If you enjoy *The Fall of Western Man*, you are encouraged to download the digital version and share it among friends and colleagues.

First Printing: 2017
ISBN 978-1542417648

www.thefallofwesternman.com

CONTENTS

ACKNOWLEDGEMENTS

I would like to thank my family and friends who have helped me with this work and supported me throughout my career.

Special thanks to:
Stephen Fyfe
Scott
RT
A+J

Cover photo by:
Sandro Goretti

FOREWORD

This book seeks to paint broad brush strokes and illustrate larger trends within Western society. It is written with the backdrop of Western civilisation being on the brink of collapse and Western man rapidly heading toward being a minority in his own homelands. These points are not debated or laboured, for one only needs to look at demographic data or view news reports to see how the racial and cultural make-up of the West has dramatically changed over the last few decades.

This book does not seek to tread the typical and well-worn ground that has been gone over time and again. This book does not seek to blame the downfall of the West on immigrants, but instead on the changes that have affected Western man and caused the breakdown of Western society. Immigration obviously leads to demographic problems as mentioned earlier – but it is not immigration that has fractured the Western communities.

Instead this book seeks to analyse how Western man has gone off track and lost his way. It seeks to analyse the mental state of Western man and show how the enemies of the West have subtly affected the Western psyche. This book lays bare the ways in which negative influences and degeneracy have been repeatedly pushed upon Western man and used to undermine once cohesive societies.

This book uses illustrative quotations and examples to illustrate the degeneracy that has been foisted on the West; however there are so many examples that listing them all would be excessive. The reader is free to, and encouraged to, apply the logic herein and find their own examples that can easily fit the framework of the arguments. If one tried to list every single example it would fill dozens of books – and to quote Shakespeare, 'Brevity is the soul of wit'.

Equally, this book is not concerned with listing names of people that have pushed such degeneracy on the West. Again, this would be unproductive and could easily fill dozens of books. The reader is again encouraged to carry out their own investigations into who 'the enemies of the West' are.

The purpose of this book is to analyse the ways in which Western man has been misguided and lost his way and the way that structures that once held Western society together have been undermined and eroded or perverted.

1
THE ID, THE EGO AND THE SUPEREGO

The id, the ego and the superego are the three component parts of the human mind present in Freudian psychology. These three distinct parts of the mind (or psyche) interact with one another to influence the way we behave and moderate the way we go about interacting with our environment and other individuals within that environment. Freud argued that the id, the ego and the superego affect decision making and guide us on a particular path based on our needs and how we should go about satisfying those needs.

Before each of these components are discussed and understood, it is important to realise why we must understand them. The id, the ego and the superego and the modern understanding of our psyche were developed by Sigmund Freud (born Sigismund Schlomo Freud; 6 May 1856 – 23 September 1939). Freud was an Austrian neurologist and is acknowledged as the father of psychoanalysis.

Freud's work forms a basis for understanding how our minds work – and to understand the working of the mind is to understand how we as human beings work on a mental level and is the key to understanding what drives and dictates our actions. Once one understands how the complex human mind works, one can see how the working of the mind can be influenced and altered, and thus how the manipulation of the mind can be used to change the behaviour of an individual person or group of people.

The key to understanding the mind would give any person or group of people a powerful advantage over others. This advantage would allow those people to use subtle and coercive techniques in order to not only influence the mind, but also to influence the behaviour of the people whose minds were being influenced. In effect, to understand the mind would unlock the secrets to controlling people – not through force, but through more devious and subtle means.

Once the working of the mind is understood, an unscrupulous group could easily use this knowledge in order to place mental chains upon people or to unleash the worst mental aspects hidden within the psyche of those people in order to ensure their servitude or their destruction.

Equally, to understand one's own mind and the way it works is to give the individual the key to the mental chains placed upon them. To understand one's own mind would be to understand how one could be manipulated and in turn how one could seek to avoid that manipulation.

It is no secret that the Western world is in decline and it is also no secret that Western man has lost his way. Yet why is this – why has the once mighty Western man who explored and conquered the world been reduced to so little in such a short period of time? Popular explanations will range from and include government policy, liberalism, socialism, immigration and even factors like unemployment. These are all however external influences on Western man.

The purpose of this book is to assert that it is not simply changes in Western man's government, it is not changes in the make-up of his homeland nor is it changes in his environment that have truly broken what made Western man great. It is in fact subtle and prolonged changes in Western man's mind that have taken place over the best part of a century that have altered the way in which Western man's mind works.

This subtle manipulation of Western man's mind by his enemies – those who wish to see the West crumble – has altered the behaviour of Western man and has both robbed him of the traits that made him great and strong, and at the same time unlocked and fed negative traits in order to make him degenerate and weak. The enemies of the West have not attacked Western man in an overt and physical way, but in a devious series of attacks aimed at the mind.

Only by understanding the way the mind works and by having one's eyes opened to the mental attacks on the Western psyche can one ever seek to steel themselves against those attacks. To understand the mind is the very first step in building that defence. By understanding the mind one can then learn how the mind is attacked and begin to see those attacks and hence start to be able to build a defence against them.

To save the West and to save Western man, the quest begins in the understanding of what makes us who we are. This quest starts with the understanding of the id, the ego and the superego.

The Id

The id is the first part of our psyche; it is present from birth and constitutes our natural instincts and drives. These drives and instincts are inherited and present in every child. These drives are made up of the driving forces for life, drives such as the need to eat, the need to sleep, the need to drink and the wish to reproduce and satisfy our sexual needs.

The id is the impulsive part of our psyche and thus it is subconscious. The id responds directly to instincts and thus unchecked it pushes the human mind toward rash and impulsive decisions in pursuit of immediate satisfaction.

When the id is satisfied we experience pleasure, and when it is denied we experience displeasure, discontent or pain. Freud described the id as operating on the 'pleasure principle' which is the idea that every wishful desire of the id craves immediate satisfaction, regardless of the consequences.

As such, the id is not affected by the realities of the everyday world. It does not on its own consider morality or logic or even physical safety; it is simply a primitive drive that seeks to satisfy basic needs and pleasures. It is often irrational and orientated toward the immediate moment and the satisfaction of whatever particular want is greatest at that moment.

To draw an analogy, the id is concerned with satisfying immediate drives and fulfilling the pleasure principle. Take in this example hunger. If the individual is hungry the id wishes to satisfy that hunger by obtaining food. The id only cares for satisfaction; it only cares for meeting that need as quickly as possible. Once the id sees its goal it will move to achieve that goal in a relentless and unconstrained manner until the hunger is satisfied.

The id is the completely unconscious, impulsive, childlike portion of the psyche that operates on the 'pleasure principle' and is the source of basic impulses and drives; it seeks immediate pleasure and gratification.

The Ego

The ego is the next part of our psyche and constitutes what is referred to as the 'reality principle'. In effect, the ego moderates the id with a view to what is realistic. The ego too wishes for pleasure, it wants the id to be satisfied and wishes to pursue the natural drives and instincts, however it will moderate behaviour and often forgo the pursuit of pleasure if it means avoiding pain or negative repercussions.

Essentially, the ego is concerned with creating a viable path to satisfy the id. It wishes to ensure that pleasure is obtained, but at the same time ensuring that any negative consequences of pursuing and attaining that pleasure are avoided. The ego is concerned with survival and is a realistic drive orientated toward problem solving.

The ego is not however concerned with right or wrong. The ego does not care for morality; it cares simply to ensure the id is satisfied, but that such satisfaction is achieved without causing harm to the individual and thus compromising the continued survival of the individual.

To continue the analogy, if the id is hungry, the driving force is to desire and obtain food. The id will relentlessly pursue the goal of satisfying that need by obtaining food. If the id sees its goal and can obtain what it wishes for, the overriding force is to move to take that food and satisfy the immediate need. However the ego keeps the id in check and questions whether it is safe to pursue that goal. In this example of needing food, if the id desires food and sees a tasty steak it will move to claim that steak, but at the same time the ego will assess whether that move is safe and will not result in harm. If the steak is unguarded and can be claimed without causing harm to the individual, the ego will let the id pursue its goal. However if the steak is being guarded by a large vicious dog the ego will attempt to override the id and postpone the pleasure in order to protect the individual and promote long-term survival over immediate satisfaction.

The Superego

The superego is the final part of the psyche. It is not based on natural drives or on reality – but instead based on morality. It is something that is learned and develops over time and is also something that is unique and differs between different cultures and racial groups as it is imparted by the community to the individual.

The superego is primarily imparted by parents and strong role models within the community. The superego functions in order to control the impulses of the id and works to control those impulses within the moralistic framework of society based on the learned morals that have been imparted to the individual.

Freud stated that the superego works on two separate levels – conscience and ideal self.

The conscience makes the individual feel bad and punishes the psyche for giving in to the id. The conscience stops the individual doing things that society would deem wrong or negative in order to ensure the individual conforms to the norms of that society. The conscience is essentially what can be described as guilt or shame. If the id demands pleasure and that pleasure is something that harms others or breaks the moral boundaries that have been learned, then the superego prevents the individual acting toward that pleasure through feelings of guilt or feelings of shame for one's actions.

The ideal self is the second part of the superego. We learn the superego from our parents and role models whom we ultimately wish to emulate and who help us form an imaginary picture of how we should be. We try to live up to those ideals and the actions of our role models to satisfy the ideal self. This has a two-pronged effect on the mind. If we fail to live up to the ideal self, again we feel guilt and shame and the psyche is punished. But the ideal self also feels pride, so when we do live up to the expectations of the ideal self and behave in a proper and moralistic fashion we feel proud of our actions and the psyche is rewarded with positive feelings.

Thus the superego both punishes the individual and praises the individual in order to allow the individual to reason on a moral level.

In order to illustrate the effect of the superego and how it works alongside the id and the ego, we will again return to the analogy of feeling hungry. If the id desires food the natural instinct is to satisfy that hunger. If an individual is hungry and sees a child with a loaf of bread the pleasure principle kicks in and the id's natural impulse is to take the loaf of bread for itself. The ego, or reality principle, will be consulted – the child is weak and an easy target and presents no viable threat so the green light will be given for the individual to take the loaf of bread and satisfy the id. However the superego then kicks in – the learned moral values tell the individual it is wrong to steal, it is wrong to take from a child and it is wrong to physically dominate another in such a way. Feelings of guilt flow through the psyche and the superego stops the individual taking the bread despite the natural drive to satisfy hunger being present – because taking the bread is the morally wrong thing to do.

The id, the ego and the superego work in this manner on a daily basis to keep us from making the wrong choices and to ensure our pleasures and natural drives are satisfied but in a way that doesn't endanger us or break the moral codes of the community in which we live.

The understanding of the id, the ego and the superego is a basis for the understanding of our mind and of how it works. This model shows in a very basic fashion how we reason and how we make choices in our everyday lives. Make no mistake; the enemies of the West have used this understanding to undermine Western man.

For Western man to ever break free and fight back, he too must understand the working of the mind and become immune to the ways in which his mind is being manipulated.

2
THE IMPORTANCE
OF THE SUPEREGO

The superego is the most complex part of the psyche. It makes us who we are and it constrains and regulates our natural urges. Without the superego we would simply be animalistic creatures who seek only to survive and pursue our natural instincts of satisfying whichever immediate pleasure we craved the most at any given time.

The superego is different from the id and the ego in one key and defining manner – it is learned by an individual and passed down to future generations by parents and role models. It is not a natural instinct but a highly complex set of learned morals and values which guide the individual, helping the individual to rise above their base animal instincts and become a developed person.

The id, as explained earlier is simply a set of natural drives or pleasure principles which demand satisfaction. We are not taught these and they are not learned; they are innate drives. They deal with immediate needs and wants on an almost animalistic level. The id is childlike and demands instant gratification.

The ego is the reality principle, the part of the psyche that tells us if a course of action is safe and reasons with the id only on the grounds of safety and whether pursuing pleasure brings the individual into unnecessary danger. The ego does not reason with the id on grounds of right or wrong or on a moral basis; it is simply a way of stopping the id putting the individual in danger.

The superego is the morality; it reasons with the id on a moral level and is thus the highest level of mental reasoning and mental development. It also follows that a developed superego or strong sense of morality across a group of people is actually the key to a smooth running and well-functioning society as a shared sense of morality is what binds any society together. When a strong superego is imparted to children, they grow up to be moral upstanding individuals who share a set of societal norms and morals which is the stuff that binds groups, communities and nations together.

Without the superego we are little more than individuals who seek only to pursue pleasure and survive and strive only for ourselves – not for the good of a group or with an advanced social conscience.

A society is held together by shared beliefs and a sense of moral duty. The closer the values are of those living in a community, the more cohesive that community will be and hence the more likely that community will work together toward common goals.

A society or community that works together toward a common goal is one that succeeds and advances. A society made up solely of individuals who pursue their own selfish ends and goals is one that fractures into smaller interest groups – ultimately at its worst becoming a loose collection of disparate individuals who only want what is best for themselves.

As stated earlier, the defining factor that makes the superego stand out from the id and ego is that it is learned. It is imparted by parents to their children – specifically and traditionally a strong and dominant male father figure has been the one to impart discipline, order and moral law to his children.

In a natural, loving two-parent family, the father is often seen as the 'stern one', the one who hands down the punishments and who gives the moral lesson and is in effect an authoritarian figure. How many times have you heard a mother say – 'just you wait until your father gets home' – this is testament to the role of the father. When the child misbehaves, the father disciplines the child and instils a moral lesson into why one shouldn't behave in a certain manner.

The mother imparts other things that help build the superego. She imparts love, compassion and empathy and more often than not is the parent a child decides to run to when hurt or upset. The mother is also an important role model for young females and plays a vital role in passing down female traits.

Thus two-parent families, specifically ones with a strong father figure, have been the cornerstone of strong societies. Youngsters who have grown up with order and discipline from a strong father figure and love and compassion from their mother follow a path similar to that of their parents, choosing to emulate them and follow in their footsteps. Children from strong upstanding families are more likely to go on to be productive members of society and work toward the common good of that society by upholding existing moral codes.

Whereas DNA passes down physical and biological traits from parent to child, the imparted superego is the way morality and shared values are passed down from generation to generation. A complete human being is not simply a group of cells and tissues, but also a highly mentally-complex life form that is able to pass down far more from generation to generation than simple biological traits.

When parents pass down their superego to their children, they are passing down more than just morals. They are passing down who they are, their way of life, their traditions, their outlook, their heritage and generations of knowledge that bind the future generations to those of the past. This allows a sense of history and tradition to be retained and passed down to future generations.

It is clearly advantageous for a society and the individuals that make up that society to have a sense of shared morality that stretches back over generations – as this not only binds people together but also helps form customs and traditions which build a rich heritage that helps strengthen society's bonds even further. This shared heritage binds the old to the new and allows traditions held dear by one's ancestors to live on and flourish in the modern day.

Primarily the father and the mother are responsible for passing down these morals and traditions in the home, but strong societies also develop additional role models that help shape the young. Teachers, scout leaders, community figures, religious leaders and other upstanding role models all played a vital role in the development of young people. As young people grew up and left the home they found themselves surrounded by strong individuals who would impart advice, morality and discipline where necessary. These individuals are role models who would teach, nurture and ensure the next generation developed along the right path.

Further to this there were other healthy role models that emerged on a national level – role models who emphasised hard work, diligence, dedication to a cause and strength. These role models were athletes, painters, writers, inventors, explorers, great military heroes, captains of industry and the men and women who built and shaped Western nations in a genuinely meaningful sense. These national role models were held up in schools and by the entire nation as beacons of virtue.

The combination of a strong nuclear family with loving parents, additional role models within the community and outstanding national role models who excelled on an unprecedented level ensured that future generations would develop a strong and healthy superego.

Just to recap, the superego is made up of two different facets – the conscience and the ideal self. The conscience is the part of the superego that makes us feel bad if we do something which conflicts with our moral code. The moral code is passed down by parents and other role models who directly imparted law, order and discipline as well as compassion and empathy.

This allowed future generations to know right from wrong, but crucially to feel guilty when they thought of doing wrong. By making someone feel bad if they consider doing wrong, it moderates behaviour and prevents the wrongful act ever taking place. The feeling of guilt kept the id in check, so the natural drives of the id were always under the control of the superego which helped ensure people did the right thing, and when people do the right thing by one another societies are more cohesive and run more smoothly.

The second part of the superego, the ideal self, is the vision we have of what we would like to be if we were at our best. Our ideal self is based on a perfect vision formed from different facets of people we look up to – our role models. So if a man's role models were healthy athletes, it is reasonable to assume that the ideal self would be a vision of strength, health and reach for sporting achievement. If the role model was an inventor or scientist then the ideal self would strive to be studious, hardworking and diligent. If the role model was a doctor then the ideal self would yearn to be patient, caring and understanding.

An important part of the ideal self is also gained from a child's parents. So if a child comes from a loving family with a hard-working father, a caring mother and an orderly and disciplined home, that child would most likely wish to emulate that later in life. Again, the strong and positive role models – both in the home, the community and on a wider national level – caused young people to strive for a strong and developed ideal self that emulated the healthiest, most productive and the best examples that Western society had to offer.

When individuals develop strong superegos and have shared morals it allows them to function as a society – a place where everyone looks out for one another and shares the same common values and goals. A strong superego also helps to create a strong vision of the ideal self, something noble to strive for. When a group of people have similar visions of an ideal self, or their visions of the ideal self have strong common facets, it is a recipe for a strong society and for community cohesion.

Whilst the id or pleasure principle is constantly pushing us to pursue the things we enjoy and give in to our natural urges, a strong superego overrides this. Instead of simply chasing a life of hedonism, we search for higher meaning and forgo the calling of the id in order to achieve more and realise a higher form of being – an ideal self.

So not only does the superego impart morality, it binds us together; it causes us to strive and to aim to attain more, something that moves society forward and causes it to develop and flourish. The superego also binds us to our past, to our heritage, traditions and ways of life. The developed superego ensures we move down the right path and continue the good work of our ancestors. One can clearly see that the mental building blocks of any civilisation are individuals with highly developed superegos.

The notion of these shared ideals and moral values across Western society gives rise to the theory that whilst each individual has their own superego – the community also has its own societal superego. Society's shared morals, traditions and heritage are what

16

bind us together and what society seeks to pass on to the next generation of that society, in effect giving rise to the notion of a collective consciousness or collective superego.

Western man has developed his own distinct collective superego – the Western superego. The Western superego guides society and holds it together; it embodies Western tradition and culture and is the very root of Western heritage. From the Western superego sprang forth the great achievements that moulded and shaped the Western world.

The enemies of the West know that Western man's strength lies in the fact that he formed a strong culture and set of traditions which in turn allowed Western man to build a cohesive society that worked in such a harmonious manner that it built the greatest civilisations the world has ever known.

The enemies of the West also know that to assault Western civilisation and Western culture head-on would be fruitless and would invariably end in crushing defeat. However if the mind of the individual was attacked, if the individual superego was undermined, then eventually the Western superego too would be weakened. Once the Western superego was weakened, the very collective consciousness of Western man and the glue that bonded individuals together and made them a community would begin to falter, and the cohesive, strong and moral Western society would start to fracture.

The enemies of the West have embarked on a mission to attack the psyche of Western man – their aim is to see the destruction of the Western superego in order to fracture Western society and bring about the fall of the West.

3
THE PERFECT
SOCIETY

The perfect society can be defined as a homogenous group of people who come together with shared morals, shared values and wish to move forward as one, working together for the good of the community whilst not forgetting the rights and importance of the individual. This community cohesion relies on a shared sense of consciousness held by the people who make up that society.

As discussed earlier, the id is the pleasure principle. It pushes people to pursue selfish, individualistic and hedonistic goals. A developed superego keeps the id in check; the superego is the morality, and when a group of people share the same morals and code of ethics they will be more readily able to form a society.

When individuals in a society adopt moral and ethical codes that are similar, it ensures that said society is more likely to succeed as the individuals in that society are more likely to move in unison to achieve goals together and to advance society for the greater good. The shared moral codes and traditions that have been passed down by generation after generation of Western man have given rise to a shared form of consciousness known as the Western superego.

Conversely, a society made up of lots of different groups and individuals who are solely focused on the selfish pursuits of individualistic happiness and hedonism is destined to crumble. If a society had no shared consciousness it would cease to be cohesive and would no longer work as a well-functioning group.

To draw a simple analogy – imagine two groups of people each set a simple task, to pull a large stone to a destination.

The first group has a shared set of beliefs and a common goal. They are bonded together as a group and care for each other. They view the importance of the group and the task at hand at a higher level than they view their own individual goals. These people are all pulling in the same direction, assisting one another and taking up the slack when necessary. Despite the task at hand being overwhelming, they will achieve their goal through their dedication to both the task and to the group.

The second group is just a loose collection of individuals. They are governed by self, by their own individual desires and all put their own self-worth above the notion of any group. They all believe the stone should go in different directions and no one sees any reason why they should strive to pull harder than the next person in the group or ever take up the slack. These people argue, they pull in different directions and their selfish and individualistic nature causes them to put less effort in than the next person in an attempt to ensure a lesser share of the work.

This is of course a very simple analogy and one painted with broad brushstrokes, but it illustrates a point – societies with common goals function far more effectively. Homogenous societies where everyone has common bonds, a shared belief system, shared goals and most importantly a common set of morals and guiding beliefs – or a shared and developed superego – work more efficiently. Homogenous societies with a shared and developed superego move forward as one, down a singular path with a clear and defined goal.

This is not only seen in humans, but also in the animal kingdom where the most successful communities are organised in colonies. These colonies are homogenous and pull together; the colonies are organised to work as one and put the good of the colony above all else. The inhabitants of these colonies do not jostle for position but work together; they pull in the same direction for the greater good.

Take a look at a colony of bees. The beehive is a highly organised structure. The queen, the drones and the workers all have distinct roles. But they all work toward one common goal – the good of the hive. The workers carry out separate duties – cleaning the hive and the comb, feeding the brood, caring for the queen, making orientation flights, building the comb, ventilating the hive, collecting pollen and guarding the hive. However the bees go about their duties with the common goal of the protection and improvement of the hive. The bees that are charged with collecting pollen do not one day decide to strike and demand to go on guard duty. The bees making orientation flights do not decide to just fly off for their own pleasure and pursue a lazy day in the sun. The highly organised and successful colony does not think of the individual – it is the colony that matters. It is this way because the individual cannot exist without the colony; the colony and its continued survival grants the individual shelter, protection, food and ultimately life.

The closer a group of people are to one another in terms of shared beliefs, moral values and traditions, the more they will work in unison for the common good and for common goals.

When one looks at societies throughout history that have gone on to be great nations, societies that grew and developed and went on to change the world, those societies have always been held together by common bonds and have moved in unison and worked like a natural colony. Whether one looks at ancient Rome, the Japanese Empire or the British Empire, when the people of these nations worked together as one cohesive group, they reached for the skies and changed the world leaving behind legacies that are still marvelled at today.

Hierarchies will always exist in these great civilisations – but the important factor for success is that those at the top are moving in the same direction as those at the bottom and both wish to advance society for the good of the group. Those at the top develop, invent, inspire and lead. Those at the bottom work, go to battle and build. But the pyramid, the simplest form of any hierarchy, moves as one in the desired direction.

The inventions, the strategies, the leadership skills, the art, the poetry and the industrial organisation of those at the top of society enable those at the bottom to be more effective, to be inspired and work more efficiently. Equally the hard work, the dedication, the commitment and the zeal of those lower down in the hierarchy is the motor that keeps the colony moving forward – and the happier and more fulfilled those at the bottom are, the quicker the motor will turn.

Equality is not the basis of a smooth-running and well-functioning society. In any successful society there is always a division of labour and the existence of structural hierarchies, just as there is in the natural world. However in a good and strong society, those at the top and those at the bottom have equal respect for each other and realise that they both depend on each other – so they move in unison as a well-oiled machine.

In a colony of bees, the worker, the drone and the queen are not equal. They are different and all have their own role to play in the colony. However their roles are all important and they work together to achieve those goals with one overriding thought pattern – the good of the colony.

In human terms and in relation to the superego, those in the hierarchy who abuse those beneath them are defectives as they have not learned a social conscience. Equally, those in the hierarchy who wish for an easy life and don't want to put any effort in and don't want to do their duty are equally defective, as they have not developed an ideal self and are not striving to better themselves.

The superego is of course made up of two different aspects – the conscience and the ideal self. They work to ensure that each individual pursues a path of self improvement in order to be the best they can, but also to have a social conscience and feel guilt when they break the moral code of the society in which they live. What is more, the shared consciousness present in society ensures that those within society think as one and the individuals who make up society all act for the good of the whole before they act for the good of themselves.

Bearing this in mind, it is quite clear that when society breaks down due to greed, selfishness, a lack of morality, laziness and the drive for individual gain – all of which are pursued at the expense of the wider good – it is due to a defective superego in the individual and a breakdown of the wider community consciousness.

The individuals who are failing the group are giving in to their id; they are putting their own pleasure principle above the wider societal morals and good of the group, which means ultimately that they have a weak superego. As individuals pursue their own agendas this of course represents a weakening of the societal superego as those who make up that society no longer share the same values.

A developed superego causes the individual to think of the group before the individual thinks of itself. This selfless outlook is a rejection of both capitalism and of communism.

A developed superego rejects capitalism on the grounds that in capitalism all that matters is wealth and the generation of that wealth. Capitalism is an economic system in which money and material gain is put above the good of the people. Individuals seek to maximise profit in a capitalist model – even if that means acting in an immoral way. In capitalism ultimately the worker becomes a slave and is worked as hard as possible for as little as possible for the short-term financial gain of the individual that sits above the worker in the hierarchy. The good of the worker is rarely considered, just the profitability of the company – the worker is seen as just a disposable resource.

Capitalism is a product of the failed superego based on a lack of conscience. It allows the greedy to absolve their guilt and give into their id to pursue profit and pleasure at the expense of others.

Equally, a developed superego rejects communism. Communism views all as equal, but equality exists nowhere in the natural world and is simply an unnatural human construct. By making everyone equal, it means reducing everyone to the level of the lowest common denominator. The removal of anyone in the hierarchy who is above the lowest level only leads to a society without direction that eventually stagnates. Communism denies that one man may have a different role in the hierarchy to another and that any man may be above another.

Communism is a product of the failed superego based on jealousy and the lack of ideal self. It plays on the minds of the jealous who, instead of striving for the ideal self and wishing to improve themselves, wish to pull down others in order to make themselves feel better.

Both capitalism and communism amount to nothing more than economic systems that the enemies of the West promote in order to enslave and corrupt Western man – one promotes materialism, the other promotes false equality. The worst characteristic of the capitalism vs communism argument is that it is presented as a straightforward choice between two absolutes leaving the individual forced into choosing between the lesser of two evils. However that choice is an illusion as there is a third way – productive enterprise.

The developed superego rejects both capitalism and communism and seeks productive enterprise. The developed superego seeks a hierarchy where those at the top have a social conscience and those at the bottom wish to rise and to achieve an ideal self and move up in the hierarchy. Productive enterprise rewards those at every level of the hierarchy and allows people to rise and fall through the ranks of the pyramid based on ability and effort. Productive enterprise thinks of the good of the group, not the good of the individual – but by putting the group first every individual ultimately benefits.

In productive enterprise those at the top are kept in check by social conscience and they aim to improve conditions for those at the bottom. Those at the bottom pursue their ideal self and wish to rise up the pyramid and because of this strive and work hard. In effect, those at the bottom push up those at the top, whilst those at the top simultaneously pull up those at the bottom. The pyramid rises and everyone benefits, everyone has their place and everyone thinks of the good of the group above their own personal interests. By this action, society advances and no one is left behind.

As in a colony of bees, despite the job specification or the level of the hierarchy the individual is at, all do their best. When all in the colony move in the same direction and individuals choose to dedicate their all, the bees move forward as one and advance the colony. There is no jealousy, no resentment and equally there is no abuse of position at the top nor laziness and greed from those at the bottom. The queen depends on the worker just as the worker depends on the queen.

A perfect society is one based on shared moral values. It is like a colony where those at every level work for the good of each other and the advancement of society as a whole – not selfish individuality and greed. A perfect society is a homogenous society – a place where the members of that society have common bonds, traditions and a shared heritage. A perfect society is one where the individuals that make up that society have all come from a similar place and move as a cohesive group toward the same destination.

In a perfect society the people look alike, think alike and act in unison, constantly moving forward and advancing as one. It is almost as if a perfect society is in itself an organism – an observation that fits perfectly with the idea of collective consciousness and a society wide superego. As such, a perfect society holds respect for its past, its culture and its traditions and builds a rich heritage passed on from generation to generation. This heritage is what bonds generations together.

A perfect society moves forward as a hierarchy, where those at the top and the bottom have a strong bond and mutual respect and care for one another. This is productive enterprise. In a perfect society individuals come together and as a result the group that is formed becomes more than the sum of its parts. This in turn allows great feats to be achieved that could not be accomplished by individuals working alone.

Perfect societies build mighty civilisations. Disparate groups of individuals achieve very little of lasting worth. The perfect society is a product of a strong community consciousness. The Western superego is the perfect example of that strong community consciousness and its achievements are plain for all to see.

4
THE IMPERFECT
SOCIETY

If the perfect society is made up of a homogenous group of people who come together with shared goals, common bonds and a binding moral compass, and who work together toward a common end and put the good of the group above the good of the individual, then what would an imperfect society be?

Firstly it is important to note that no society is truly perfect. Within any society there will always be individuals who have a defective superego, and who as a result act purely out of self-interest. The actions of those individuals motivated by self-interest often work to the detriment of society or others within that society. There will always be those individuals who lack social conscience, individuals who seek to rise above others and then exploit them. There will also always be individuals who wish to languish at the base of society and simply do as a little as possible; these individuals lack a sense of duty and ideal self. Those individuals who lack a sense of duty are lazy and strive for nothing, opting to do as little as humanly possible whilst attempting to leech off the hard work of others.

Even in the most noble of societies, both the greedy and the lazy have always existed. But what is important is that a healthy society does everything it can to eliminate those traits in people before those traits grow amongst the populace and become common enough that they start to harm the functioning of society itself.

A healthy or perfect society does everything to enable individuals to develop their superego in order to ensure that people control their id and work within a framework of moral values, hence preventing people from simply pursuing immediate pleasure and selfish gratification. This pushes people together as a cohesive group where they work together in harmony for the greater good of society.

An imperfect society however is one in which the society is no longer homogenous and no longer cohesive. This can occur for two reasons – firstly the homogenous group of people that make up the society lose their bonds with one another and no longer form a cohesive group, instead becoming a loose collection of self-interested individuals. Secondly, one or more other homogenous groups can be introduced into what then becomes the wider society, meaning that society is no longer made up of one cohesive group, but several different groups all with their own distinct interests and ideals.

We shall return to the analogy of bees.

Imagine if a beehive (in human terms the hive itself is analogous of the wider society) actually contained several separate colonies of bees (the colonies in this analogy are equivalent to separate and distinct groups living together within a wider human society). Each colony (human group) had their own idea of the way the beehive (the wider society) should be constructed, the way it should be run and each colony had self-interest and as a consequence wanted the lion's share of the honey. Not only would this not work as nothing would get done, but the different colonies would constantly be altering the work done by each other in order to shape the hive differently – this situation would be actively counterproductive. Further conflict would soon arise between the colonies living in the same hive as each vied for a greater share of space, resources and a greater share of the honey. In effect, each colony would want the hive to be run in the way they thought best and for the good of their colony. Rather than being pulled in one direction, the hive would be split and dragged in opposite directions.

This analogy seems like utter madness! After all, different colonies of bees with different ways would never try to live together in one hive. It simply would never happen as it is an obvious recipe for disaster and would no doubt lead to the death of at least one or more of the colonies and eventually result in dominance by the strongest over the weakest. Yet that is exactly what happens in the imperfect society – different groups of people are forced to live together within the same wider society, and each vie for a better deal and for more control for their respective group.

The single homogenous group that society used to be entirely composed of is altered by the introduction of other groups of people with different cultures. Society, which used to be composed of one homogenous group, then becomes a wider society, a body composed of several different groups, each with their own traditions, morals and cultures. The breakdown of the wider society then occurs as a product of different groups all wanting what is best for themselves, often at the expense of the other groups within the wider society.

In the perfect society, homogeny is the key to the smooth running of that society. Instead of this, in the imperfect society there is no racial and cultural homogeny – the imperfect society is based on multiracial and multicultural models where different people with different values, different cultures, different traditions and different heritages are forced together into one wider society. It is not just that the groups that compose the imperfect society are different, but often these groups are actively pulling in opposite directions. This leads to the wider society being pulled apart as different groups vie for control, power and a greater share of resources.

When we discussed the superego earlier, it was noted that parents, community leaders and role models pass on the superego in the form of a conscience and the image of an ideal self. Across a homogenous group this creates traditions and culture stemming from a shared sense of values and morals. This forms a community-wide consciousness as previous generations pass down their traditions, culture and heritage to the next generation.

But as stated earlier, in the imperfect society there are several different distinct racial and cultural groups. Over time each of these distinct groups have developed traditions and values which have built a shared heritage which is then passed down to their offspring. Each different group has their own community consciousness that is different and separate from the shared consciousness of other groups within the wider society.

Morality and values are not universal across the world. In fact they differ greatly from one cultural group to the next. As the values and morals that are passed on differ between groups, these separate groups develop different traditions – in effect they develop their own distinct culture which is not only different from but often conflicts with the cultures of other groups.

In the perfect society values and morals are universal and they bind the whole of society together, and that society then possesses a shared consciousness – for Western man that is the Western superego. But in the imperfect society which is composed of many different groups, many different and often conflicting value systems exist – this prevents those different groups mixing and bonding and in turn prevents the wider society functioning as one cohesive body.

In a multicultural or multiracial society, there exist lines of nonconformity which stem from different groups having different heritages, traditions and value systems. Individuals identify most strongly with others who are like them. As a result people choose to remain loyal to their own group and their own group consciousness rather than to any notion of the wider society. The different groups within the wider society all have their own traditions and values that their constituent members identify with above and beyond the traditions and values of the other groups within the wider society. Often this leads to friction between groups as values and morals clash.

Shared values are something that is possible, but a move toward shared values and conformity between different groups is a move toward the deterioration and dilution of each individual group's culture and cultural standards. This is often termed 'integration', but to integrate one culture into another means compromises must be made, which inevitably means giving up or diluting parts of one or both of the different cultures being integrated.

Think again of the different colonies of bees. As several different colonies of bees now have to share the same hive, the bees of each separate colony stick together and choose to remain around their own. Each bee within the hive identifies with the dances and the queen of their own colony. Each bee yearns to be with his own and serve his own and further the goals of his own colony. This leads to competition and conflict between the colonies and a desire amongst each colony to dominate the others. If one group of bees decided to adopt the ways of another, if one group of bees started serving another's queen or doing another group's dance, it would lead only to that group losing its own identity and eventually becoming extinct as an individual group. That group would have effectively been conquered, not by warfare but by assimilation and submission. It would be seen as highly unnatural for the bees to do this though, as in nature 'birds of a feather flock together'.

It is natural for creatures to identify most closely with other creatures of their own species that look familiar and act in a familiar manner. People feel safe around others who not only look like themselves, but also who act like themselves because they share the same morals and values and have the same interests and ways of life. The traits passed down through our DNA allow us to identify with others based on our racial or physical appearance. The shared morals passed down, that over generations become traditions, allow us to identify with one another based on other learned factors – the way we dress, the way we behave, our language and our shared value system.

In a multicultural or multiracial society, not only do people look different, but they dress differently and have different values, different traditions and different ways of life. So it is natural that we seek out those like us and cluster together with our own, feeling more at home and happy around our own where we can enjoy the comforts of being around others like us.

That is why the analogy of a wider society that is composed of many different groups being like one big melting pot is simply a fantasy. The reality is people on the whole like to stick with their own – after all that is their natural calling. Hence in multicultural and multiracial societies different cultural groups cluster together rather than choosing to mix with another. Areas in cities and towns can be defined by the people living there, people who are part of one wider society, yet have made the conscious choice to live in closer proximity with those who share similar racial features or cultural ties.

As different groups refuse to integrate with one another, instead opting to remain as separate and distinct entities in an effort to retain their own culture, tensions often rise within the wider society. Each group wants a better deal for their own people. Whereas in the perfect society people pulled together and worked toward common goals and pulled in the same direction to achieve a better life for everyone, now different interest groups pull in their own directions and want a better deal for their own group – often at the expense of the other groups within the wider society.

One group wants a community centre for their cultural needs. They lobby, they demand, they petition and eventually the squeaky hinge gets the oil. Religious buildings, cultural centres and other services are built to serve that particular group – but are of little or no use to other groups within the wider society. People from particular groups then cluster around areas where their community is better represented, where their needs are better catered to and where their community centres, religious buildings and shops are closer.

As time goes by ethnic and cultural lines are drawn across the wider society and people increasingly stick to their own areas – feeling out of place when they venture into an area dominated by another ethnic or cultural group. As a result, people move nearer to their own group and seek to put distance between themselves and groups they don't feel at home living next to – the effect is akin to trying to mix oil and water.

A society that was once completely homogenous and composed of just one cultural group can quickly be transformed into a patchwork quilt of different people and cultures that are largely separated in their own areas. The cohesive nature of society has now been broken – replaced instead by many smaller and individually cohesive units, each rubbing against one another as they vie for dominance within the wider society.

As the different groups in society pull further away from one another and continue to move in their own direction it is no longer simply a matter of separate groups jockeying for position in order to try and get a better deal for their own. Over time these groups begin to take exception to the other groups present within the wider society and demand laws to ensure that their way of life is respected and adhered to by others. Sooner or later these factors lead to increasing tensions and even conflict between different groups within the wider society.

But introducing other groups into a homogenous society is only one of the two ways that society can be broken down – the other way this can occur is if people that make up a homogenous group lose their bonds with one another and no longer form a cohesive group, instead becoming a loose collection of self-interested individuals.

Now imagine what would happen in a multicultural society composed of many different cultural groups, if one group was undermined. Imagine if as each different cultural group sought to retain their cohesiveness and came together to secure a better life for their group, one group started to lose their common bonds and community consciousness. Imagine if one group, instead of fighting for the good of its own people and acting like a colony, became just a loose collection of individuals. Imagine if – as every other cultural group present in the wider society pulled together with their own – one group instead chose to increasingly spurn its own culture and the individuals within that group sought self-interest rather than putting their own community first.

Imagine what would happen to the group that showed this weakness. That group would surely disappear; they would disintegrate and no longer exist as a cohesive community, leaving the people who once made up that group as helpless individuals. Those individuals would then face the choice of either being absorbed into one of the other different groups within the wider society and taking on that group's culture, or they would simply go it alone and be slowly bred out of existence.

For this fate to befall a cultural group, that group would have to lose its shared sense of consciousness – or its shared superego. This could of course be achieved by attacking the structures within that group that kept it strong and allowed it to pass down its shared superego from generation to generation. Ultimately this would represent the death of that group's values and with it their traditions and heritage. The values that bound that group together would weaken and the group would fracture – and as a result the individuals who once comprised that group would either be assimilated into other cultures or die out.

This is the way Western man's enemies have plotted his downfall – by simultaneously introducing other cultures into the West and creating an imperfect, or multicultural society in which many different groups all vie for dominance. Then by undermining the Western superego and Western man's sense of community consciousness, that ties him to his brothers and sisters, the enemies of the West have sought to leave Western man as a helpless group of individuals rather than a community that can defend itself.

Western man's fate is then clear – to be bred out and be assimilated into other more dominant cultures.

5

THE RISE OF THE ID AND THE FALL OF WESTERN MAN

The id is the completely subconscious, impulsive, childlike portion of the psyche that operates on the pleasure principle and is the source of basic impulses and drives; it seeks immediate pleasure and gratification. The id has no conscience and no view toward the wider good of society. The id only cares for the immediate short-term needs of the individual.

It is clear then why the id needs to be controlled – why it must be kept under the watchful guard of a developed superego. If the id was to triumph and have complete control over the psyche, the individual would be reduced to an animalistic beast that lived only for the immediate pleasure of the moment and have no conscience for the wider good of the community.

The enemies of the West know all too well how the human mind works and are using this knowledge against Western man – they seek quite simply to free the id from the constraints of the developed superego. By freeing the id, the enemies of the West seek to reduce Western man to a group of self-interested individuals, who when placed within the wider confines of a multicultural society do not have the group consciousness or cohesive nature necessary to survive as a distinct people or cultural group.

Let's look carefully at how this could happen: Imagine a group of people who were once a homogenous and tight-knit community – a people with an advanced set of morals and values that had developed into deep rooted and highly complex traditions and a long illustrious heritage. We know that those people would pass down their morals and values from generation to generation as parents and role models helped to impart a developed superego into the next generation of society.

Now imagine if over a period of forty or fifty years a generation gap occurred, a gap that prevented the superego being handed down from one generation to the next. Imagine if parental control over the young and the structures within a society broke down meaning that the young grew up without discipline or positive role models. Imagine what would happen to those people if they no longer constrained their id with a strong and moral superego.

Imagine if that group of people stopped passing down their traditions and cultures and instead the young were left without a sense of the heritage that had held those people together as a community for all those previous generations. This would surely not only destroy the individual superego, but also the shared morals and values that exist within a cohesive community.

Imagine if the group that was losing its sense of community and was losing its community-wide superego lived within a multicultural society, and was surrounded by other groups and other cultures – all of whom sought to retain their culture and heritage and remain as individual and distinct cohesive groups.

The group that possessed the weakened superego, and the group which was composed of individuals more likely to give in to their individualistic needs and wants and their basic primal drives for selfish pleasure, would lose its sense of cultural homogeny and as a result that group would fracture. The individuals within that group would pursue individualistic needs that would put the very existence of the group at risk.

This is the fate of Western man. Western man has allowed millions of immigrants into his homeland, immigrants who have a culture, a sense of togetherness and who wish to retain their moral values and sense of community. These immigrants still retain their superego and pass it down from generation to generation. These immigrants cluster together as distinct communities and seek to retain their culture, heritage and religious practices. At the same time, Western man has slowly seen his superego become weakened and distorted. The consequence of which is that the id has increasingly been allowed to dominate the Western psyche.

Western man has become increasingly individualistic and Western communities have become fractured and disparate. The bonds that held Western communities together and the trust and love between Western man and his brothers have been broken as successive generations have followed the need for immediate selfish pleasure above the need to protect the group and do what is best for Western society. As the individual's superego has slowly weakened, so has the sense of community consciousness.

This is the aim of the enemies of the West – to unleash the id and see Western man be reduced to mere animalistic beasts – animalistic beasts that could neither build nor defend a civilisation. The promotion of animalistic desires and instant gratification is of course not something the enemies of the West find difficult to push upon Western man – after all, how difficult can it be to persuade people to have fun and let their obligations and cares drift away?

It is even easier to convince someone that the path of hedonism is the correct route to take when their moral compass has been smashed. But how have the enemies of the West gone about smashing the Western moral compass? The enemies of the West have smashed Western morality and values in numerous devious ways, all of which undermine a different key facet of Western society.

Western man has witnessed the rise of the fatherless family, a place where children are brought up without the advice, order and discipline provided by a strong father figure – a place where mothers abandon their offspring to go partying. These women then go on to have children by multiple men in a desperate search to satisfy the id's craving for sexual hedonism. These children are then often left to be brought up by the television and end up lacking both a conscience and a healthy image of an ideal self.

Western man has witnessed the destruction of the safeguards in Western society. Western schools and community role models are now powerless to dispense any form of discipline and children run wild – instead of developing a superego, the child simply does as it pleases and learns the fatal message that happiness and instant satisfaction are all that matters.

Western man has seen his role models go from being great men and women who shaped society in selfless and awe-inspiring ways, to being drunks, cheats, drug users and degenerates. Young people idolise false role models who constantly give them the message that all that matters is to 'party' and have 'fun', that living for the 'now' and the 'self' is all that counts – and after all, if it doesn't feel good, why do it? The sense of ideal self that is imparted by these role models is now a twisted version of what the ideal self should be and children grow up with a warped sense of what is right and what should be strived for.

Natural barriers and boundaries have been broken down and the natural order of things has been turned on its head. Feminism has created a world where the woman who follows her natural instincts and becomes a loving and caring mother who nurtures her children is looked down upon and scorned. As a result children are now left without a loving mother – the very person who imparts conscience and guilt.

Feminism has attacked the two-parent family, telling the woman she doesn't need to stay with the man she fell pregnant to and that a father isn't important. This has left the Western world with children who don't have a father, with young men that grow up believing they don't need to be a father and young women who grow up believing they 'don't need a man'.

Feminism has pushed women into the workplace, and the natural and fulfilling roles of being a mother and homemaker have been pushed to one side. Women are encouraged to follow masculine career paths and engage in futile attempts to outperform their male counterparts. This leaves the Western female with a reduced birth rate as women pursue material goals rather than the spiritual ones that have served Western man so well for generations and have held Western society together.

As a direct consequence of feminism the male has become emasculated. The male is no longer the alpha, the provider and the strong cornerstone of the family or the community. The male now cowers beneath his female; he begs, cries and fails to satisfy her as the natural gender roles have been reversed. Young men have increasingly become the weaker sex as they have failed to learn order, discipline and strength due to an absence of a strong father figure or other strong male role models.

The Western mind has been corrupted and the Western body has been broken and grown obese and useless. Western spirituality has been lost and replaced with wanton materialism. But most shockingly, the Western heart has faded and the bravery and courage that Western man showed in abundance when defending his people is now a thing of the past.

Rather than being a strong group with cultural, racial and moral bonds – strong traditions and a rich heritage – Western man has given in to the pull of hedonistic individualism where people live for themselves and the immediate pleasure they can gain in the short term.

As the Western superego has weakened, the id has been unchained. As the id is no longer constrained the individual lives for selfish pursuits and immediate satisfaction – whether that is food, sex, alcohol, material wealth or drugs. Is it any wonder that those who come to Western shores and see Western man engaging in such debased and degenerate acts then view the Western world as a place that is ripe to be taken and conquered?

Western man's hedonistic lifestyle is the physical embodiment of the rise of the id. But with the rise of the id comes the fall of Western man. The oft heard phrase; 'fiddling as Rome burns' seems apt. But in a more modern sense – Western folk are partying, drinking and having endless promiscuous encounters as Western civilisation crumbles and the West is slowly colonised by an endless stream of culturally hostile immigrants.

The rise of the id is present before the collapse of any civilisation. Every great nation or civilisation that has collapsed has embraced the cult of individualism, and the individual has been increasingly motivated by the pursuit of endless and immediate pleasure.

This is of course exactly what the enemies of Western man have planned. The enemies of the West understand the complex working of the human mind and realise that to break a community and turn that community into a group of disparate individuals all that needs to be done is to convince those people to give in to their immediate desires.

Even with immigration and multiculturalism, the enemies of the West knew that Western man would still have a fighting chance of survival – in fact better than a fighting chance. Even if Western man was outnumbered by hostile cultures and peoples, as long as Western man retained his own culture and sense of community he could always fight back – and if history has taught us one thing, it is that Western man would likely have prevailed.

It was not merely enough to flood the Western world with different groups of immigrants who viewed the West with envious eyes. The enemies of the West knew that the Western community spirit – the Western superego – must also be broken in order to ensure there would be no fight back or resistance.

The last thing Western man will see is the look of insane mirth upon the faces of the Western revellers as Western civilisation, culture and traditions collapse and are lost forever. Thousands of years of heritage will be lost in a matter of decades as the last generations of Western man compete in a desperate struggle to live for the moment and satisfy their every primal need with no thought for the future or the wider consequences their actions might have for the West.

The enemies of the West know that the rise of the id precedes the fall of Western man, and they sit rubbing their hands and biding their time as the final days of the West rapidly approach.

6
THE BREAKDOWN –
SINGLE PARENT
FAMILIES

The developed superego is the key to a well-rounded human being. The superego develops during a child's upbringing and is the only learned part of the psyche. The superego is the morality and the values that prevent the id from embarking on an endless pursuit of immediate and animalistic satisfaction. The development of the superego goes on throughout childhood, beginning at an early age and moving forward into the teenage years as the child matures into an adult.

It would be accurate and correct to state that the development of the superego is largely down to the child's parents. During childhood the people a child most closely identifies with are his or her parents. The child spends an enormous amount of time with their parents and the parents have a huge influence on the child's mental development.

The superego is made up of two separate entities – the conscience and the ideal self. The conscience is what punishes the individual with feelings of guilt if they pursue something that is morally wrong. The ideal self is the perfect vision of what an individual should be; it is an ideal which that individual then strives to live up to.

Bearing in mind the dual nature of the superego and the vast influence the parents have on a child's development, it is obvious that defective parents or bad parenting could easily stunt or completely damage the development of a functioning and well-rounded superego in a child.

Further to this, if one parent was missing from the family unit there would be huge repercussions on the children as each parent imparts different components of the superego to the child. The absence of either parent would leave a child without a balanced upbringing as the child would lack either the male or female perspective.

Before we go on to discuss just how damaging single parent families are to the development of a child's superego, it is first important to look at how crucial the nuclear family has been to the development of Western man and how the family unit has always been the cornerstone of Western society.

Europe, especially Northern Europe, is a cold and harsh place for large periods of every year. If one was given the option of being dumped naked anywhere in the world in December with no tools, resources or food, Northern Europe would logically be one of the least favourable destinations one could choose. The ground is frozen, the nights long, the leaves have long fallen from the trees and the birds and fish have migrated south.

Europe can be a beautiful and lush place at the right times of the year, but in winter it is a harsh and unforgiving place – and one that would have severely tested Western man's early ancestors. Let us take this hypothetical situation a step further, and imagine a woman and her child being dumped alone in Northern Europe in December, with no tools, resources or food.

Caring for a baby or small child is difficult at the best of times – but when dealing with the harsh elements as well as a lack of food, resources and long cold nights it would be almost impossible for a single parent (male or female) to bring up a child alone. Yet, those are the conditions in which Western man evolved and ultimately flourished. As Western man is still here today, it is obviously true that his ancestors managed to succeed at surviving through the long, hard winters and that they were effective at raising and protecting children during these trying times.

The obvious answer to how Western man's ancestors managed to survive and raise children is that they did so as a couple. Those who came together as a couple and those who formed lasting bonds were much more likely to see their children survive through the winter months. Conversely, men who abandoned their women or women who ran from their men would most likely see their offspring perish when the seasons changed and the conditions got harsher.

Nature's law is survival of the fittest and over time the evolutionary pressures on Western man were clear – those best adapted for survival were those who adopted the early model of the nuclear family. This nuclear family would become the cornerstone of Western life.

With the birth of the nuclear family came the division of labour. The male became the hunter gatherer and the female became the early homemaker. The male left the shelter in search of food and resources and specialised in tasks such as hunting, tool making and foraging. The female remained behind and learned skills that evolved into what we know today as multitasking.

The male would go out each day and typically pick one particular task to do at once. He would specialise in that task and develop it in isolation from other tasks. Whether that be the creation of tools, hunting animals, fishing or gathering resources – the male would do each of these tasks on their own, as attempting to do them all at the same time would lead to catastrophic failure. One cannot hunt whilst at the same time trying to create the tools with which one is supposed to hunt.

The female stayed in the dwelling and developed a totally different set of skills which gave birth to the female art of multitasking. The female would cook, clean, tend to the young, organise the dwelling and keep feeding the fire with fresh wood. None of these tasks required constant attention for long periods of time in the same way the males' tasks did. The female would move from task to task and learned to balance doing many things at once.

In essence, the male and female complemented each other as a pair. One dealt ably with one set of tasks whilst the other dealt ably with another. The male and female form what is clearly a complementary pair whose roles are unique, yet complement each other's roles perfectly. Essentially the male and female formed a partnership and together that partnership was more than the sum of the respective parts that it was composed of. The nuclear family was born and developed from that point on.

The family unit became a selective advantage for Western man and the division of labour and natural healthy gender roles flourished. Western man's children survived and their genetics were passed on to the next generation. Those who could not find a complementary female or those who abandoned their partner were highly unlikely to have offspring that survived their first winter, their genetic line was erased and a strong precedent was set.

Even at this early stage of Western development, the superego was being passed down from generation to generation and those with the strongest superegos were more likely to prosper. Although Western man was living in caves and using animal skins for warmth, the Western superego was starting to flourish, that spark was starting to create the traditions and values that shaped Western nations and Western culture into what they became at the height of Western civilisation.

Back in the days of the hunter gatherer, the same battle took place in our primitive minds – the id, the ego and the superego existed. As always, the id pushed for instant gratification and pleasure, the ego added the reality principle and the superego added the early forms of morality.

The earliest moral value was to form a family unit and protect one's partner and offspring. This initial bout of conscience, which involved not letting your partner and offspring struggle and starve to death, coupled with the early ideal self which was clearly to be a strong hunter, provider and reliable partner, shaped the male into a dominant father figure who was strong, dependable and the cornerstone of the family unit – a protector and an authority figure.

This evolved into the modern Western family unit where the male assumed the role of a fatherly figure that gave advice, dispensed discipline and order and was the head of the household. These early moral values can also be credited for the creation of the loving, dependable and caring motherly figure – a woman who is loyal to her partner, her children and committed to supporting both. The ideal woman was loyal to her partner as he was loyal to her and the more motherly and caring she was and the more children she bore the more likely it was that her bloodline would flourish.

However those that followed their impulsive pleasure principle, those who gave into their id and simply pursued selfish gratification and hedonism were unlikely to survive and their offspring never had a chance. Those who went it alone for an easier life and put themselves first either died alone or their children never reached maturity. Their DNA was lost in the passage of time and their bloodlines came to an abrupt end.

The children of the early nuclear family saw this. They were born with their id, but they soon developed a strong superego. They saw their mother and father together; they saw the division of labour in early Western society and they developed a conscience toward their parents, siblings and the fledgling community that surrounded them. They developed feelings of guilt for letting down their family and community and they developed the first and earliest form of ideal self – they wished to emulate their mother and father and follow in their parents' footsteps by raising their own family.

Both the male and the female would be brought up in a two-parent family environment. The young females would learn from their mother in the dwelling and the young males would soon leave the dwelling and go with their father to learn how to become men.

Crucially, the male is the key disciplinarian for both young males and young females. The male acts as the head of the family unit and is the strong alpha and as such his role in the family is to dispense any form of judgement, discipline and order within that family. As such the female and other younger members of the family would turn to the male to settle any disputes and keep the family in line.

The female's role was that of the caregiver. She would give attention to the young, the wounded and the ill. She showed compassion and love and nurtured a different form of development. Both the male and the female imparted equally important values to future generations making both a mother and a father crucially important in the upbringing of children and the formation of the child's superego.

As Western society advanced and went from families to tribes, and from tribes to nations, the leaders of Western society noted the importance of the family unit. The family unit was enshrined in law – and the idea of divorce was heavily frowned upon with those wishing to split apart their family unit being scorned and treated as outcasts.

This trend was further cemented by religion: all religious texts talk of the importance of the nuclear family and of the union of man and woman. All those who wrote such texts realised that the strength of a people lay in the strength of their family bonds. So it held that religion also strengthened the family, again frowning on divorce and promoting the family unit.

Such was the importance of the family unit and a loving two-parent home, that should a woman fall pregnant, the man was expected to marry her and create a home with her, and both the male and female were to come together for the good of the children to ensure the successful upbringing of the next generation. The superego stated that the pleasure of the two individual parents was less important than the welfare of the next generation.

At one point it would have been unthinkable for a single parent family to exist – unless through the sad loss of life of either partner or a genuine reason for divorce. Divorce was always frowned upon and wedding rights were rightfully thought of as a union for life which was only to be broken when 'death do us part'.

However, as stated earlier, there is no such thing as a truly perfect society and in every society there are flawed individuals – those who give in to their id and pursue instant pleasure at the expense of the good of others, whether that is the good of their friends, society at large or the good of their partner and family. Divorce should obviously be a last resort, but in certain cases it should clearly be granted.

These limited cases are fourfold: Firstly in the case of genuine sustained abuse – whether physical or mental. No one should have to live in an abusive relationship. However abusive does not mean being shouted at once in a blue moon during an argument, nor does it mean the occasional push or shove. Every relationship will have its ups and downs, and a slight down period that leads to an explosive argument should not be used as an excuse to undo months or years of good, productive and loving companionship.

Secondly, infidelity – which should not be tolerated in relationships or within society. The growing acceptance of infidelity is a direct result of the breakdown and weakening of the superego. The id will always want satisfaction and always crave more satisfaction. The superego should be strong enough to forgo that satisfaction on the moral grounds that one has a partner and is married. An individual should never put thirty minutes of pleasure before the good of a lifelong relationship. If an individual cheats, then they are not suitable to bring up children as their actions are indicative of a weak or defective superego. As the cornerstone of Western society, the family comes first and those willing to break it for instant gratification are not suitable to bring up children.

Thirdly, genuine irreconcilable differences are grounds for divorce. A genuine irreconcilable difference would involve an individual going off the rails for a sustained period of time and as such their actions would present a threat to the continued wellbeing or even the existence of the rest of the family. The wayward individual's actions would be detrimental to the family's continued healthy lifestyle – for example, if a partner begins gambling, taking drugs, becomes an alcoholic or takes up another wholly negative pursuit which places the family unit in jeopardy. However, before the relationship is broken, a responsible partner should do everything in their power to help steer their wayward partner back in the right direction. Relationships are hard work, and couples should not give up on each other at the first sign of trouble.

Finally, the fourth reason for breaking up a marriage is if a parent presents a threat to the couple's children. The importance of a two-parent family is to ensure the correct upbringing and protection of the children. However if either side of that bond – the male or the female – becomes a threat to those children then that indeed would be a strong reason to break up the marriage as it would defeat the very purpose of the union. If two people come together to protect a child, but one of those two people intends to harm that child then the union is indeed pointless and counterproductive.

However today breaking a marriage could not be easier – in fact the divorce rate in many Western nations is now over 50 per cent. People get married, have children and break their vows over the most petty of things – with divorces within the first year of marriage becoming ever more common. It is as if for some the marriage itself is not worth the piece of paper it is written on; marriage has now become more about holding a lavish and materialistic wedding in order to show off to friends and family and less about making lasting vows that should represent an unbreakable bond between two people.

For many the urge for marriage no longer centres on love and moral vows, but from the immediate gratification of a giant party and the attention surrounding the wedding ceremony. This has been fuelled through trashy magazines, television shows and the constant coverage of celebrity weddings – most of which seem to collapse in record time. Increasingly the drive for marriage simply represents another way to show off and gain short-term attention; this is not only a corruption of the institution of marriage, but also of the traditional ideals that underpin marriage.

Marriage has been reduced to such a joke and marriage vows are so easily broken, that the importance of marriage has waned in the mind of the Western man. There is now less of a drive for marriage – even if a woman falls pregnant. The idea of a couple being expected to marry if the female fell pregnant would seem positively 'old fashioned' and 'out of touch' and those putting forward that opinion would be scorned.

But with the breakdown of marriage comes the rise of the single parent family. The cornerstone of Western society, the nuclear family, has been broken. What took thousands of years to evolve through natural means and then was enshrined in both religious and state law has been dismantled in a matter of decades. Western morality and values lay shattered and the family unit is broken up so individuals can pursue their own selfish pleasure.

This leaves Western man in a situation where mothers bring up children alone and there is no father present in the home. Increasingly the mothers in question have multiple children by multiple men, and the older children are forced to watch different men coming in and out of the home as if that were natural and healthy. The adults in these relationships are only bothered about satisfying their immediate sexual urges – in effect gratifying their id. These individuals have a weak superego and do not remain together to care for their young as those with a strong moral compass would.

We now see generations of children who are brought up without a father – the individual who was once the head of the family unit. The father as discussed earlier was the strong disciplinarian – the individual in the household who imparted authority and order, the one the family unit turned to for strength, protection and guidance.

The father figure plays a key part in the development of his child's superego and helps impart a sense of ideal self; the father is both a role model and a teacher. But increasingly he is no longer present. It is no coincidence that an increasing number of children – both young males and females – are tearaways with little or no care for authority, order or discipline. These feral youths walk the streets late at night, indulge in poor practices, skip school and generally seek only their own pleasure.

The id has claimed these youngsters, because they lack discipline in the home and lack a father figure to look up to as a role model. But the problem with single parent families doesn't end there, that is just the beginning.

Once the single parent family has been allowed to thrive and become a social norm, the values that were once held across Western society begin to crumble. At one point it was necessary to bring up children as a couple – simply for survival. Every child that survived its first winter did so because its parents had worked together. The two parent family was then enshrined in religious and state law through the act of marriage. Marriage is now mocked and the laws surrounding marriage have been progressively weakened.

Society no longer sees the nuclear family as normal or as a desirable ideal. The very sense of ideal self – a fatherly male and a motherly female that was imparted to children as part of their developing superego is lost. The ideal self is no longer centred on attaining a partner and building a strong family. The ideal self becomes a warped and defective version of what it is meant to be and the superego gives into the id's desire for individualism and pleasure with little or no regard to the upbringing of future generations.

The nuclear family which is the very cornerstone of Western society is under sustained attack. Children and the well-being of future generations are no longer put first; instead selfish individualism becomes the goal. Moral duty has been thrown to one side in order that everyone can 'do as they please'.

As a consequence Western society is now littered with feral children who do not respond to their elders. These feral children lack strong role models in the home and as a result look for role models elsewhere. These lost children are searching for someone to look up to and admire, someone to act as a model for their vision of an ideal self. Now imagine just what would happen if these lost children were then presented with bad role models. Imagine the catastrophic effect on their young minds if when searching for a suitable role model, they came across false and destructive role models who further warped their sense of right and wrong and led them further away from the right path.

Not only would they stray further, but they would lack any fatherly guidance in the home and more importantly they would lack the discipline and order necessary to pull them back in the right direction. This would surely be a recipe for future generations to stray totally off track and become completely lost.

The bonds built from generation to generation and passed down from father to child would be broken. Tradition, culture and ultimately heritage would be forgotten. By breaking apart the family unit, the enemies of the West have achieved the first step toward breaking the bonds between Western man and his ancestors, and as a result tens of thousands of years of development and culture stand to be lost.

.

7

THE BREAKDOWN –
THE REMOVAL OF
SOCIETY'S SAFEGUARDS

The nuclear family is the cornerstone of Western society. It developed as a necessity, as an evolutionary advantage to ensure the survival of the next generation of Western man. The loving mother and strong father formed a lasting bond and were able to pass down not only their DNA but also their shared morality to the next generation in the form of the superego. Children were brought up with a sense of ideal self that centred on emulating their parents and forming a similar family when they matured.

But Western society is much more than just a loose collection of individual family units. Whilst it is true that the nuclear family is the single most important aspect of Western society, society itself also plays an important role in shaping the development of the young. Many individual nuclear families make up a society, and in that society there are other role models, teachers and disciplinarians that impart rules, moral guidance and tradition to the next generation.

This has been true of Western society even back in its infancy when Western man struggled in the frozen wastes of Northern Europe. Even in those harsh times, many families came together and formed tribes. In those tribes leaders emerged – men who were the strongest, the wisest, the best at hunting, the fastest and the best at creating tools and so on. Those individuals shaped the tribe and became another set of role models who would help children develop their ideal self outside of the parental structure and would impart new skills, traditions and values upon them.

These role models within society also acted as a safeguard. As stated earlier no society is perfect; there are always defective individuals – people who will put their own individual pleasures above that of the good of the group or even above the good of their own family and offspring. These individuals live for their id as they have a weakened or wholly defective superego. So as tribes formed, a safety net was put in place to ensure that no member of the next generation would fall through any cracks that may emerge.

If a family unit broke down and a mother was left alone – whether that be through a defective individual with a lack of conscience abandoning her, or through tragedy as her partner died, her children would not be left without a strong male role model as these role models were also present within society.

Equally, females developed their own structure within the tribe and women were admired for their beauty, motherly attributes and their skill at bringing up children and keeping an orderly home. These women took up a matriarchal role which moulded future generations of young women into ideal mothers through developing a positive female vision of the ideal self.

If, for one reason or another, a child was left without a mother, women within the tribe would take on the role of that child's mother. This meant that no child would go without a positive role model and that positive role models within the home were reinforced by positive role models within society.

At the dawn of Western civilisation, these role models would have taken more primitive roles. The young males outside of the home would have looked up to the leader of the hunting party or the male who taught them how to build and use tools. The women would gather with young girls and taught homemaking skills such as the making of clothes and how to tend to infants. This further reinforced what was learned in the home and impressed on the young that listening to their elders and emulating those elders was important.

All of these factors brought the tribe together and built a strong superego in future generations. The sense of collective conscience grew as the importance of the tribe grew – it was a shared sense of morality and survival meant looking after one another. Those who did not pull their weight became outcasts and were shunned. Hence a sense of guilt was formed; this guilt punished the id if the individual thought of pursuing selfish pleasure above the good of the group.

Equally, the other constituent part of the superego, the ideal self, was also moulded into shape. Through strong two-parent families, fatherly discipline and role models and teachers within the community, children would look up to healthy, loving and strong individuals who all were placed in high regard due to their skills and commitment to the tribe. The Western sense of ideal self started to take shape in the image of an individual who pushed for the good of society and was selfless, strong and moralistic.

As Western civilisation began to grow so did the shared values within society and the birth of the Western superego was witnessed.

Skip forward to the height of Western civilisation and the safeguards in society were made even stronger. As time advanced, layer upon layer of role models, safeguards and fail-safes were put in place to mould and shape future generations and pass down traditions, values and Western morality.

Through a mixture of schooling, religion, law, the workplace, community groups and strong community leaders, young people had positive role models wherever they turned. Society was geared toward the rearing of the young in such a way that the next generation were intended to be better than the last and move society ever forward – embodying the spirit and heritage of the past with a view to an even brighter future.

Now imagine a society where those safeguards are broken down and dismantled, a society where instead of common bonds that tie different family units together into a cohesive society, those common bonds are eroded. Where generation after generation does not have the tribal leaders and role models, but instead the young are left to listlessly go their own way and develop by themselves. Imagine a society where healthy role models, pastimes and community groups are scorned and mocked and the strong, ordered and dignified industries have closed leaving future generations with little or no purpose.

The Western school system was one of the first and most important safeguards in society. Basic schooling and teaching has been with us since the days of the cavemen – when parents taught their children survival skills and the early tribes had their elders, master craftsmen and most skilled hunters pass their knowledge onto the rest of the tribe.

These teachers not only passed on skills, but became role models and authority figures to the young. The young looked up to them and wished to emulate them and learn from them in their quest for their ideal self. This evolved over thousands of years into a school system – a place where every child had a right to a standard of education, a place where basic numeracy, literacy and other important skills were taught to all in order to raise the quality of life in society as a whole.

A perfect society was described as a pyramid; a place where those at the top pulled up those at the bottom, as those at the bottom simultaneously pushed up those at the top – in essence a society where everyone sought to ensure that the overall standard of living in that society increased for everyone. Nowhere was that more prevalent than in the early education system.

Schools did not just teach children, schools provided children with discipline, order and role models. Schools were a place where children could learn and further understand the structures of life – but importantly a place where, if discipline was lacking in the home, children could further develop their superego under the supervision of their teachers. School was one of the most important safeguards in society.

At the height of Western civilisation, schools were a place where children learned, a place where children looked up to their teachers and a place where children understood discipline and order. That has now been turned on its head. Robbed of their power, mocked in the mainstream media and with discipline and order removed from them, schools have become a place where children pick up bad habits and learn to scorn Western culture and hate their own ancestors.

Teachers are no longer seen as role models or authority figures – as they have no power and are afforded little respect. At one time a truant child, who ran away from school to pursue a pleasurable day of play, would soon learn from both teachers and parents just why following the path of the id was not acceptable. Swift discipline would have been meted out. But now truancy, disorder in the classroom and even teachers being attacked and belittled by their students is the order of the day.

Rather than a place of learning where the superego is reinforced, the school has become a place where fewer and fewer safeguards lie in place and more and more youngsters drift off into the pursuit of pleasure, giving into their id without a thought for the consequences. This of course stunts the growth of a child's superego leaving the child without a conscience or a sense of ideal self.

Religion was another substantial safeguard in society. Every Sunday families went to church as a group. The church was a place that was important not just for imparting moral values and traditions, but as a place that brought entire communities together as a group and reinforced the tribal nature of Western society.

The religious leader of the group also became another one of society's role models. The religious leader dispensed moral and spiritual advice and the young listened to his sermons and learned important lessons. As spiritual leaders, those in the clergy emphasised the importance of family, the importance of the married couple and the importance of a community where individuals could trust in one another and depend on one another in difficult times. Just as the school presented discipline and intellectual teachings to the children, the church presented discipline and spiritual teachings.

Again the sense of ideal self and group conscience was reinforced. The repeated message was that the family, marriage and community were fundamental to any well-running and well-meaning society. Moral laws were passed down – do not steal, do not covet thy neighbour's possessions, do not covet thy neighbour's wife, along with many other teachings that kept people on the correct moral path. The church also presided over marriage and frowned heavily on divorce in a concerted effort to keep families together.

The church was another institution that emphasised the development of the superego and scorned the idea of immediate and hedonistic pleasure.

Today the church is a shadow of its former self. Many churches lay empty and abandoned and the churches that do remain open see religious leaders preaching to an ever decreasing flock. Just as the school system has embraced a lack of discipline and the teachers have lost their authority, so have the religious institutions fallen from grace. Churches have liberalised their message and religious leaders have become a mockery of what they once were.

The church has not only dwindled in terms of the size of its congregation, but it has become defective and riddled with the same liberal poison it once preached against. It is no coincidence either that the further the church has strayed from its own moral teachings the more people have turned away from the church. The church no longer presents a strong and healthy moral voice that people can turn to in times of need. Instead the church is weak as it has chosen to embrace the poisonous mantra of those who wish to see the West crumble.

Most churches are now frequented by older generations, people who still go out of duty and because of what the church once was. The younger generations are totally absent – in effect another place where the young would develop their ideal self and a community conscience is now distant to them.

Western civilisation also had strong and moralistic laws and those who upheld the law were seen as beacons of the community and were trusted by all. The police were once seen as role models, people one could trust and people one could turn to. The local officers were respected and formed another important stratum of discipline and order within society that young people could learn from.

The traditional role of the police officer was as a protector of the community. As stated, no society is perfect and even at the height of Western civilisation there were still defective individuals and criminal elements – but by and large due to the developed superego and social conscience and strong community bonds people were free of crime and looked after one another.

Times were once so peaceful and crime free that people didn't lock their doors as they didn't fear burglars or thieves. The sense of community instilled in people was generally so strong that the community conscience present in society prevented people from harming their neighbour and the sense of ideal self people developed would have been far from the image of a common thief.

It followed that police officers were a presence that often dispensed advice and simply kept a watchful eye over communities. If the young strayed in minor ways they would simply be given a harsh talking to and returned to their parents, who naturally would be ashamed and discipline them further. Thus the lawman was seen as an upstanding individual – one that was held in high regard and would have contributed further to a youngster's vision of an ideal self. The law was something that people adhered to, and those who upheld that law were respected and looked up to.

Almost the opposite is true now. There is huge distrust and division between the police and communities and as such the law and those upholding it are no longer held in the high regard they once were. Police no longer represent a friendly face that everyone in the community knows, and people certainly aren't eager to leave their doors unlocked anymore.

The police no longer seem to have powers to deal with criminal elements, but have plenty of time to chase parking fines and harass those who speak out against the liberal political narrative. The police have become disliked and as such the law and those who uphold it are no longer the role models they once were. But that in itself presents a problem – if the young are presented with an officer of the law that is distrusted and disliked, his word and the discipline it carries is no longer effective and no longer seen as just. Another layer of order within society is broken.

A developed superego looks up to and admires discipline and seeks to emulate it. A developed superego creates a vision of an ideal self, which is a perfect vision of what one should strive to be. Police officers were once role models within the community; police officers added to and strengthened the ideal self and the conscience of society, now they do the opposite. Another healthy role model is distrusted and brushed to one side.

Outside of the classroom and the church children were also presented with numerous other healthy role models as they took part in healthy and fulfilling past times. The scouting movement, the girl guides, the sea cadets, young farmers and other clubs and groups presented young people with upstanding members of the community who freely gave their time and energy for the good of society rather than for personal gain.

These groups helped children further develop their superego and helped transform them into upstanding members of society. The virtues instilled in scouts are a fine example of how children's pastimes helped them develop into upstanding adults; the scout law is as follows:

A Scout is to be trusted.
A Scout is loyal.
A Scout is friendly and considerate.
A Scout belongs to the worldwide family of Scouts.
A Scout has courage in all difficulties.
A Scout makes good use of time and is careful of possessions and property.
A Scout has self-respect and respect for others.

What could be a better set of morals and rules for a child? The scout's law is just an example of how groups within the community would instil values and morals into young people that would strengthen and bolster what they learned from their parents and from role models in other institutions.

The other important characteristic of groups like the scouts, girl guides and sea cadets is their activities often encouraged young people to be both physically and mentally healthy and connect with nature. These groups promote weekends camping, outdoor activities, survival skills, cooking, hunting, hiking and general fitness and well-being – all of which are crucially important to the development of young people.

These groups also promote charity, fundraising and helping the community. They teach the next generation that community and social cohesion matters. They teach youngsters that selfless acts for the good of the community can earn the individual respect within that community and that respect can give the individual an inner feeling of self-worth far greater than the self-worth gained by an act of immediate selfish gratification. By teaching youngsters these important lessons these groups help strengthen the superego, build a sense of community and keep the id in check.

Sadly groups like the scouts are in rapid decline. Western youngsters are no longer presented with these healthy pastimes by society and instead choose to sit inside playing computer games and watching television. The young sit indoors having their minds poisoned, as instead of being presented with healthy role models like the men and women who lead the scouting movement, they are presented with the twisted role models that the media promote.

Yet again we see that another important group of Western institutions that help impart morality, values and traditions upon young people are in decline. But worse still, these institutions are mocked – they are made out to be 'sad' or 'square' and those who attend these groups are mocked and ridiculed, and often the media represents those who are members of such groups as 'boring' or 'odd' or 'old-fashioned'.

Instead of spending their evenings and weekends working as a group, learning important skills, carrying out charity work and connecting with nature – all things that create a well-rounded person and develop the superego – children are left to their own devices. Instead of pursuing gainful activities and looking up to upstanding community leaders, children spend their time in pursuit of selfish pleasure and individualism. This is something that if not inhibited, will result in an adult who will not ably fit into a community nor even want to be part of one.

It is not enough that there has been a concerted effort to undermine the family unit and that there has been a rise in single parent families. This in itself has undoubtedly had a huge effect on Western civilisation, after all the nuclear family was once the cornerstone of Western society. The decline of the nuclear family and the resulting lack of parental control and fatherly discipline, order and morality in the home have led to the decline of the developed superego in the next generation.

But on top of this, the safeguards that have been put in place within Western society in order to strengthen morality and community cohesion have also been removed. The very fail-safes and structures put in place that would aid in the development of a well-rounded and balanced young person have been smashed apart and are now ineffective, distrusted and even mocked by the young people they are meant to inspire.

The safeguards that would once catch the odd wayward child or youngster that came from a broken or dysfunctional home are now all but gone – and at a time when there are more fatherless children, broken homes and wayward children than ever before!

Now imagine a situation where young people who do not have a father figure and also lack positive role models in their communities are searching for someone to look up to and someone to emulate. Young people need role models, role models they can emulate and role models who help them develop their sense of ideal self.

Imagine Western society devoid of loving families, strong fathers and community leaders. Then imagine what would happen if the enemies of the West were to present the lost and confused Western youngsters with the worst possible role models – role models who would attempt to impart a warped and defective superego upon those youngsters. So that instead of pursuing a life of family, order, hard work and selfless dedication to their community the future generations of Western man instead pursued a path of individualistic hedonism and degenerate madness.

Without the family and without the safeguards in the wider community, the young would be easy targets for the enemies of the West. As the pied piper did with the youths of Hamelin, the enemies of the West could easily lead Western youth astray down a path of moral destruction and degeneracy. Then in a few short generations everything that Western civilisation has built and everything it once stood for would begin to crumble.

.

8

THE BREAKDOWN – BAD ROLE MODELS

The superego, the learned part of the psyche, is the morality and value system that keeps our animalistic pleasure principle in check. A developed superego is the part of the psyche that is good, moral and holds society together. It is made up of the conscience and the ideal self and allows us to reason on a higher and moralistic level.

The superego is imparted to us primarily by our parents. The nuclear family was the cornerstone of Western civilisation and the mother and father passed down healthy morals, values and traditions to the young. Families were tight-knit units and the parents themselves were role models to their children and their children developed a sense of ideal self based upon how their parents behaved.

The superego was then strengthened and reinforced by strong upstanding role models within the community. Teachers, community leaders, religious figures and other authority figures who imparted law and discipline all became role models for the next generation. They helped build a strong sense of conscience and all presented good ideals to which young people could aspire too.

However as different tribes and communities came together to form nations, a third and final form of role model emerged – the national hero. National heroes were people held up by the nation as great inventors, explorers, sportsmen, captains of industry, artists, writers, poets, military heroes and other individuals whose actions and achievements were of such importance that they were credited with making advancements that benefited the entire nation.

These national heroes represented the pinnacle of Western man's achievement; the best of what Western civilisation had to offer and were elevated as such for all to see. The nation's heroes became another group of role models that served to inspire the next generation and help them to develop into healthy young adults. These national heroes personified personal sacrifice, hard work and dedication to raising the standard of Western society. The national heroes were a perfect source of inspiration for children developing their own vision of an ideal self.

Take for example a great military hero like Horatio Nelson – a man who was known for his inspirational leadership abilities, his dedication to his nation and his bravery under fire. Horatio Nelson was wounded several times in battle losing both an arm and the sight in one eye, yet despite suffering setbacks that would ground and demoralise any normal man, Nelson went on to achieve victory at the Battle of Trafalgar, the final and decisive battle of the Napoleonic naval conflicts. In this battle, Nelson gave his life for his nation and for victory.

A role model like Horatio Nelson would be a powerful and worthy inspiration for a developing mind. He personified the ability to overcome hardship and ultimately to triumph in the face of adversity. Nelson showed that dedicating one's self to the good of one's nation and the survival of one's people, above the call of personal gain and personal gratification, was a noble and just endeavour. Finally, his ultimate sacrifice for the good of his nation and for victory showed a selfless man who was willing to give his all.

All of the qualities embodied by Horatio Nelson would surely be a positive set of moral codes and values for a young person to embrace. They would ensure that the next generation would see that personal sacrifice for the good of the community is a noble cause and that there is more to life than simply seeking personal gain and personal pleasure. The young admirer of Horatio Nelson would understand that ultimately the best and most noble individuals are ones who act on moral grounds for the good of their people and often sacrifice personal gain and immediate pleasure for the continued survival of their people and betterment of their nation.

National role models, whether they are military heroes like Nelson, sporting achievers, writers, explorers or inventors all sacrificed short-term pleasure to dedicate themselves to a single task that in the long term benefited the wider populace and pushed society forward as a whole and set an example to the nation.

The national role models were all individuals with great talent, but were also characterised by having highly developed superegos which were witnessed through their dedication, hard work and selfless acts. Had any of these role models given into their id and sought selfish pleasure rather than remaining steadfast they would never have achieved the things that they did and would not have lived on in the hearts and minds of future generations.

In the early days of Western civilisation national role models lived on long after their deaths as their names and achievements were passed down from generation to generation by word of mouth as communities gathered around the fire. The great deeds of the nation's heroes went on to be written down and immortalised. Songs were sung to commemorate their lives and the inspirational acts they had become renowned for. Their stories were passed down from generation to generation in this manner and they lived on in the hearts and minds of their people.

These great individuals who achieved so much became the stuff of folklore and the tales of their exploits were woven into the very fabric of Western culture and heritage. This set an example to future generations and tied Western man to the history of his people and served to remind Western man of the achievements of his ancestors.

As Western civilisation advanced, the young learned about national role models in schools and universities. Schools presented their students with the names and great deeds of the men and women who had shaped Western civilisation. These healthy national role models were held up so the next generation would not only give thanks to them for their sacrifices, but also so the next generation could aspire to be like them. These role models helped form the picture of an ideal self in the minds of Western youth.

Imagine however if the healthy role models that inspired generation after generation, the very people Western man sang songs of and wrote books about, were slowly written out of history and the young no longer learned of their achievements. Imagine if the great men and women who moulded and shaped Western civilisation were actually forced from the collective consciousness of Western man by those with an anti-Western agenda. Imagine a world where men like Horatio Nelson, Robert Falcon Scott, William Shakespeare and Isaac Newton were forgotten.

To forget one's national heroes, the very people whose outstanding contributions to the West shaped and moulded Western civilisation, would be a terrible crime. It would be a great sin as it would not only pay huge disservice to such great and outstanding individuals, but it would also alter history and the collective memory of how Western man had advanced so far. To write these people out of history would destroy part of the West's rich culture and heritage. Writing these individuals out of history would also rob future generations of a number of strong upstanding role models, men and women that should serve as an inspiration to build a youngster's sense of ideal self.

But imagine further, if when the healthy and virtuous role models who emphasised everything good in society were written out of history, that they were to be replaced with negative role models. Imagine that the replacements for the great men and woman who shaped Western civilisation were defectives and degenerates – individuals whose message to the young was not one of personal sacrifice, morality and hard work, but a twisted and poisonous message of self-indulgence, hedonism and 'do what makes you feel good'.

Sadly you don't have to imagine this scenario, as this is not some twisted nightmare based in an alternative universe or a nightmarish science fiction fantasy; it is the reality of the world in which Western man now lives.

The nuclear family has been undermined. The very cornerstone of Western civilisation has been destroyed and made a mockery of. The two-parent family that has existed from the days when Western man lived on the edge of ice sheets and that grew out of evolutionary survival pressures and was subsequently strengthened and enshrined by religion and the state has been broken. As the family unit has declined, so have the order, discipline and morality that the family unit instilled into the next generation.

Further to the loss of the nuclear family, the safeguards that society put in place for the young have been dismantled. The community leaders, the strong teachers and disciplinarian figures have all been removed and weakened to the point they are ineffectual.

This has led to a situation in the West where the young have no order, lack moral values and desperately look for role models who they can emulate. But instead of being presented with healthy and virtuous role models, they are presented with bad role models, men and women who emphasise everything that is wrong with society and who push a warped valueless message of selfish hedonism designed at undermining Western society.

One only has to look at the role models presented to young people today – the movie stars, the fictional characters on television and the big screen, the musical icons, the reality TV stars and the many other vacuous and morally devoid individuals who are held up by the media and establishment as 'heroes'. These 'heroes' are anything but real heroes; they are invariably individuals who embody almost everything that is degenerate, defective and damaging to society.

Even the few remaining 'positive' role models that actually dedicate themselves to some form of genuine greatness such as sporting achievement are tainted with vanity, caught out using drugs, abusing alcohol and cheating on their partners. In essence they are reduced to tabloid fodder as their lives play out like soap operas showcasing their flaws and chronicling their fall from grace. Even those who appear to be virtuous eventually fall from grace, and that fall and their subsequent embrace of degeneracy is always emphasised as if that is a natural and inevitable part of life.

This amounts to a highly effective attack on the Western superego as those in control of the media and the establishment push endless damaging role models and destructive messages upon a generation of youngsters in desperate need of guidance and moral fibre.

The negative message is always the same – hedonism and pleasure come first. To return to the first chapter, we discussed the id, ego and superego and the role they played in the make-up of the psyche – it was said that:

The id is the impulsive part of our psyche and thus it is subconscious. The id responds directly to instincts and thus unchecked it pushes the human mind toward rash and impulsive decisions in pursuit of immediate satisfaction.

The negative messages pushed by these destructive role models and the negative examples these role models set are all the same – give in to your natural urges, make rash decisions, be impulsive and seek immediate satisfaction. The message is always to pursue short-term happiness and to never think of the consequences.

Let us look at a few examples of the poisonous message pushed by these defective role models; the first example is a song by Lady Gaga called 'Just Dance'. Read the crazy lyrics below and take some time to think about the message they carry:

I've had a little bit too much, much
All of the people start to rush.
Start to rush by.
A dizzy twister dance
Can't find my drink or man.
Where are my keys, I lost my phone.
What's going on on the floor?
I love this record baby, but I can't see straight anymore.
Keep it cool what's the name of this club?
I can't remember but it's alright, I'm alright.

[Chorus:]
Just dance. Gonna be okay.

The message is clear for all to see. The woman singing has had too much to drink; she is acting in an irresponsible manner and is heavily intoxicated to the point of being 'dizzy'. In her drunken state she realises she is so far gone she has lost her keys (presumably to her house or flat) and she has also lost her phone. Her state is now deteriorating further; she can't see straight and has even forgotten the name of the club she is in. This is a terrible state for any individual to be in and shows a complete loss of control over oneself, it is the ultimate triumph of the id over the superego.

Yet what is the solution, what is the motto of this story – 'Just Dance. Gonna Be Okay'. That is the motto, the lesson learned. In this state of drunkenness where she has lost her keys, phone and doesn't know where she is, the only thing that matters is more hedonism and she 'just dances', because as long as she is enjoying herself it's 'gonna be okay'.

Now the reality of the matter is that it probably isn't 'gonna be okay'. Despite the medical problems associated with getting that intoxicated, the woman has lost her keys and her phone and doesn't even know where she is. The financial cost of losing a phone and the potential costs of hiring a locksmith to get you back into your home in the early hours of the morning are not small. The developed human mind would now be in panic mode and realise that a large error of judgement had been made. What's more, for a female to be that intoxicated and then for her to be separated from her 'man' in an unknown place is not safe or wise.

The strong superego is there to prevent an individual giving into to the animalistic and base desires of the id. The superego makes moral judgements that prevent us giving into the animalistic urges that reduce us to being lesser creatures. But here the imparted message to the impressionable youth is that despite everything being such a mess, one should only give in further to the id and pursue more pleasure and more gratification, after all if you 'just dance' it is 'gonna be OK'.

What could be a more destructive message to impart to young people, a more degenerate and defective role model and a more twisted version of reality? Yet the person pushing this message is a global mega star and a role model to millions of young people – in fact she has sold over 170 million albums and singles. Is this a fitting replacement for Horatio Nelson? What do you think the difference would be between those brought up with Horatio Nelson as their hero and those brought up idolising Lady Gaga? How would their moral compasses differ?

Take one more example of the destructive messages being pushed by the music industry and the twisted role models that influence the next generation of Western society. This gem is from Katy Perry and is taken from the song 'This is How We Do', another glorification of drinking and partying above all else;

This one goes out to the ladies, at breakfast, in last night's dress
Uh-huh, I see you
Yo, this goes out to all you kids that still have their cars at the club valet and it's Tuesday
Yo, shout out to all you kids, buying bottle service, with your rent money
Respect

This is an example of a role model giving direct encouragement and praise to her followers for acting irresponsibly in the pursuit of pleasure. She acknowledges the 'ladies' at breakfast in last night's dress, and what a fine example for young people – to stay out all night partying and living large. She then goes on to mention the 'kids' who have abandoned their cars at the club valet despite it now being Tuesday – presumably the weekend has long gone but the individuals are so intoxicated they have either forgotten where their car is or are unable to collect it. Finally she gives a 'shout out' to the kids buying alcohol with their rent money. She tops this off by giving these wayward youths her 'respect'.

Now imagine a national hero of old stopping by at a school or youth organisation and praising the youngsters for doing something good – for carrying out charity work, or creating something of beauty or possibly working hard to achieve something in the field of sport. Positive reinforcement and acknowledgement by role models cements in the young person's mind that what they are doing is good. A fine of example of this is when awards are given at scouting events for the groups that have raised the most money for a charity.

Drinking until the early hours of the morning is not good, especially not for young women. Forgetting where your car is parked or being so intoxicated that three days later you can't collect that car is not good. Spending your rent money on partying, essentially getting yourself in the situation where you could lose your home is utterly irresponsible and stupid and is the perfect example of how the id can triumph for immediate pleasure without any view to the future. Yet Katy Perry, an 'artist', who has sold over 100 million albums and singles and who is a hero and role model to millions, is giving her 'respect' to the young people acting in this manner. Katy Perry, like one of thousands of these negative role models, is giving positive reinforcement to negative actions.

These are just two examples, but there are countless others out there and listing them all would be pointless and exhausting. But the pattern is clear; modern role models for the next generation of Western society are giving the opposite message to the ones given by traditional role models.

Order, discipline, morality and values are scorned in favour of hedonism, pleasure and instant gratification despite what the future consequences may be. Remember, it is more important to pay table service and get drunk than it is to pay your rent, or should that be the other way around?

Instead of the national role models that the young look up to giving out advice and lessons on morality that strengthen the superego and help keep the id in check, role models now do the opposite, urging the young to give in to their base and selfish desires.

The lost youth from broken families, who lack strong role models in their communities, desperately seek to develop their ideal self, and the ideal self they develop is not ideal at all. The ideal self that is imparted by the destructive role models is literally the opposite of the ideal self that was central to building Western civilisation. It is a twisted vision of the ideal self, and is anything but 'ideal'. It is selfish, greedy, lazy, hedonistic, short term in its outlook and the very opposite of the ideal self that is conducive to a well running and cohesive community.

The key to Western civilisation is a cohesive community and a strong society. A strong superego and developed moral values build a society where people come together for the common good. Positive role models reinforce the idea that the individual should strive to do well for their community and put that community above their own selfish and hedonistic needs.

Earlier it was discussed what would happen if the bees in a hive all decided to go out and have fun and seek personal gain rather than pulling together and doing what was good for the colony and the hive. Now Western youth are taught exactly that – live for yourself and your own immediate pleasures – and this is exactly what they do. So is it any wonder that Western civilisation is tearing itself apart and losing its homogeny when the next generation is actively adopting a selfish lifestyle that is not conducive to community, positive traditions or upstanding values?

The national role models of old were virtuous individuals who helped move civilisation forward and emphasised that doing good for one's people was the correct path in life. Today's role models more often than not do the very opposite. They are vacuous and empty and push a rotten message. They are role models who cheat on their partners, abuse substances, abandon their families and stand for nothing but the pursuit of wanton hedonism.

Western civilisation now has a generation of young people who are literally regressing thanks to their lack of a developed superego. All the safeguards placed within society are being slowly attacked or have been removed; parents are no longer a partnership and discipline in the home is often non-existent and these lost youths turn to the modern-day pied pipers who lead them down the path of destruction.

But it is not just Western youth who will be destroyed due to this madness; it is Western Civilisation that will crumble as a result. What took millennia to build and shape will be broken apart in mere decades. Traditions and cultures that were passed down from generation to generation and have evolved and existed for thousands of years will be forgotten and lost. The rich Western heritage, history and Western way of life will all be washed away within a century of madness.

The enemies of the West understand that Western strength and Western culture lies in the ties that bind Western man to his past and his historic achievements. They also understand that the future of the West lies in Western youth – and by separating the two they know it spells disaster for the West.

Western man discovered and colonised the world, then went on to reach for the stars, yet the enemies of the West are intent on sending Western man crawling back to the primitive call of the id. Instant unevolved animalistic pleasure is now the order of the day as the enemies of the West seek to undermine and destroy everything that once imparted the Western superego to the next generation.

9

THE ROLE OF FEMINISM – THE DEATH OF THE LOVING MOTHER

So far it has been discussed how the structures of Western society have been dismantled and how this has affected the development of the superego, and thus allowed the primitive, selfish and pleasure-seeking id to begin to triumph, and the effect this has had on Western society. As stated earlier, society functions and works as a well-oiled machine because of shared moral values that are present within a group – in essence a shared superego that has been imparted to the young.

To this point the discussion has been very male orientated and focused more strongly on the role of the male as the disciplinarian and patriarchal authority figure in both the family unit and the community as a whole. As order and discipline is in the main dispensed by strong masculine figures, a strong father figure and strong male role models are essential for the functioning of a strong society. These strong male figures have kept society – and crucially the next generation on the right path, helping to facilitate the passing down of tradition and values.

The individuals who have advanced Western civilisation, the inventors, the captains of industry, the explorers and the military heroes have more often than not been male – but that is not to write women out of history or to diminish the role of women in society. To claim that women have been written out of history or to denigrate their contribution is to play into the hands of the enemies of the West.

To return briefly to the example of the honey bees – each bee has a role to play, whether that is the role of queen, drone or worker and regardless of the job the bee carries out, each is vitally important in its own way. The same is true in Western civilisation, the advancement of which came about through people pulling together and playing their individual role without thought to selfish gain. As no bee mocks another because of the role they carry out, no man should sneer at a woman and no woman scorn a man because their role in society may differ.

Take for example the role of the family unit and its importance to the development of both society and to the next generation – this has been discussed extensively in earlier chapters. It has been stated that the male is the head of the house – a disciplinarian and authority figure. Does that relegate the woman to being less than her male counterpart; is the wife in effect less than the husband? Of course not!

Nature favoured the male and the female coming together as a lasting and stable family unit and bringing up children in such a way because males and females form a complementary pair. Both the male and female are different, physically and mentally, both bringing different skills and attributes to the relationship. When a male and female come together they create a union that is more rounded and balanced than either individual, and ultimately a couple can be seen as more than the sum of its parts.

If the male can be described as the 'head of the house', the female could easily be described as the 'heart of the home'. The loving and motherly female was as much a central component of Western society and the nuclear family as the male, and her role as the compassionate, supportive, nurturing and loving influence on the child is as important as the discipline, the order and the authority imparted by the male.

The superego is of course composed of the two facets we have previously discussed – the conscience and the ideal self. Whilst the strong male role model imparted discipline and order which helped shape the ideal self, more often than not the conscience which is founded on empathy, love and care was born from the influence of the loving mother. This conscience was helped in its early stages of development by the bond the mother had with the child; this natural and loving connection between mother and child is vital to the early development of the infant.

The loving mother is any well-balanced child's first and most indelibly printed and lasting memory. The mother feeds, cares for, nurtures and looks after the infant child in every way, doting on the child and imprinting a lasting bond that as the child grows and develops to maturity helps the next generation remain tied to the family and the mother that raised it. This motherly bond with the child binds individuals to their family and their past with feelings of love and memories of childhood happiness that should never fade.

What greater achievement is there for a loving mother than to successfully raise her children and see the next generation of her family and blood develop into fine upstanding members of the community? What could be more satisfying to anyone than to see the child they gave birth to, fed, nurtured and taught grow up into a strong and well-rounded member of society? A strong and upstanding young adult is the physical embodiment and a living proof of a mother's hard work, love and skill as a parent.

These are natural callings; nature's most basic drives are for an individual to survive and to pass on their blood to the next generation. These acts of motherly love and child-rearing have been going on since the earliest days of Western development. Ensuring that the child was kept warm through the ice cold winters huddled in the early dwellings of Northern Europe, ensuring the child came first when it came to food, even if that meant the mother going without, ensuring that the child was protected and nursed through sickness – all of these things were the great sacrifices every successful mother made.

The female was never the 'weaker' of the sexes nor treated as such, but was a vital complementary partner to the male. Whilst the male was out hunting, gathering, fishing and creating tools, the female mastered the art of multitasking – feeding the fire, tending to the children and checking the progress of the food being prepared. The female was the homemaker – and running a successful home was no small feat nor was it less important than the tasks undertaken by her partner.

As Western civilisation advanced, the motherly figure became the housewife and her role as homemaker was cemented further. As Western society moved off the ice sheets and developed into an advanced society, the female became ever more the beating heart of the household – literally running the home as she raised the children. To pour scorn on the mother and the housewife, or to attempt to diminish the role the mother and housewife played in the development of Western civilisation, would not only pay a disservice to generations of women but it would also serve to create division between the sexes where previously there was none.

However this is exactly what has happened during the 20th century – the role of the woman as a homemaker, loving mother and committed partner has been scorned, mocked and derided by those who wish to see the destruction of Western civilisation. The same people who have facilitated the breakdown of the family unit, the same people who have removed the safeguards in Western society and the same people who have foisted unsuitable role models upon Western children have conspired to attack the natural role of the female in society with a poisonous ideology known as feminism.

Feminism is a multi-pronged attack on Western civilisation that aims to create division and distrust between males and females where previously there was understanding, cooperation and harmony. Feminism is a wholly unnatural calling that attacks the natural urge for a female to come together with a male and form a complementary pair and raise children in a loving two parent home. Feminism is not just an attack on the male as many mistake it for, but an attack on the female and her natural role. When taken to its logical conclusion feminism leaves a woman trying to emulate and outdo the males around her in a futile attempt to prove she is better at masculine pursuits than her male counterparts.

Feminism attacks the very essence of femininity. It is an attack on everything that women have achieved and the contribution of every loving mother, loyal wife and committed homemaker. It belittles the contribution of the supportive partner, the doting mother and attacks women who seek to satisfy their natural and loving urges.

The feminist battle against 'the patriarchy' or the male is seen as a noble cause for women who wish to rise up against their male oppressors – however this battle of the sexes is not a genuine fight but one manufactured by those who wish to create division and discord within Western society.

The war waged by the feminist is done so under the seductive guise of equality. But as stated earlier, equality does not exist in the natural world and men and women were never meant to be equal, but different components of a loving partnership. The woman and the man were meant to work together to achieve more as a pair than either could have achieved alone. Men and women are not meant to be at war with one another, but are meant to form a complementary pair. The male and the female are different, but are meant to come together in order to each provide the different components that make up a single entity which facilitates the successful raising of children.

In the feminist's battle to defeat the male and surpass and dominate him, the feminist knows that the female cannot be victorious by being feminine, motherly and pursuing her natural gender roles. Feminists tell women to cast off their natural urges and desires and instead emulate male attributes. This wholly unnatural process forces the woman to be like a man in order to compete unnaturally with her partner at the things he does best. Feminism drives women to throw off and discard the traits that make them unique and cherished and so very important to society.

The feminist fantasy of defeating the male on his own ground is however a difficult if nigh-on impossible task as the male and female have carried out their different gendered roles not just for generations but for tens of thousands of years. The male and female have each grown and evolved in different ways over the millennia in order to be best adapted to the roles they played – roles which due to their complementary nature are vastly different. The male developed a stronger, more muscular and athletic build to become the best hunter, a skill that in turn increased the male's spatial awareness. As discussed earlier, the female developed patience and multitasking as she dealt with many tasks at once, including the rearing of the young.

Feminism has created a dichotomy where the female is forced to compete against her male counterpart, and essentially go against her natural callings and her own highly evolved skill set. To do this she must jettison her feminine attributes and womanly ways and attempt to become like a man in order to compete effectively. But with women increasingly striving to be like men, this presents the West with another mortal blow – the death of the loving mother.

The very heart of the Western family, the loving motherly female, has now been ripped out – a casualty in the feminist's war for a false equality that is neither achievable nor desirable for a stable and healthy society. For when women try to emulate men, they lose what it is that makes them so special and destroy the attributes that make them so vital to the Western world.

As the female tries to emulate the male, the most striking change that she goes through is to discard her loving and motherly ways. The female aims to excel in the workplace and match her male counterparts, who she now competes with rather than embraces, and the casualty in all this is the female's natural motherly and loving instincts. The male is strong in different ways to a female; he is harsher and less emotional. In order to compete with the male the woman has to also become harsher and less emotional – essentially supressing and discarding the traits that made her a good mother. This transformation has a profound effect on the way a woman raises her children.

Rather than aiming to be a housewife and mother and aspiring for a large family, the female aspires to work as a male would and compete with men in the workplace. The woman no longer judges herself on the how well she manages the home and how well her children are brought up but on whether she can perform in the commercial world. This drive is directly at odds with the drive to have children.

What's more, if and when a woman does have children, her drive is now to get back into the workplace leaving the children at playgroups or with childminders. A child's early years are vitally important as it is in these early years that a child bonds with its mother through almost constant contact with her. The mother feeds, nurtures, and cares for the child and is in charge of almost every aspect of the child's upbringing, if these tasks are not carried out by the mother in a natural way, but by others who are designated to carry out the motherly tasks on her behalf, this can stunt a child's development.

Separating mother from child weakens the bonds that hold the nuclear family together. But this separation also has an effect on the mental development of the child. The conscience is part of superego; it is made up of empathy and gives the individual a feeling of guilt if they contemplate breaking the moral codes and values of society. The conscience is an important aspect of the development of a child and it is imparted largely in the early years from interactions between mother and child. A loving mother imparts those feelings and builds the conscience – a sense of right and wrong, which is obviously bolstered and reinforced by the order and discipline imparted by the father.

To remove the mother from the child in the early stages of development also increases the levels of stress on the child and can even cause a child to suffer from depression – something that can affect the development of the child both physically and mentally. This is known as attachment theory and is something that can be easily read up on and has been extensively studied. Interestingly, attachment theory states that other caregivers – be they nannies, grandparents or childminders are not a substitute for the mother. The child knows if it is, or is not, with its own mother and this affects the child's feeling of contentment and happiness and thus affects the child's mental state.

A loving mother is essential to a child's development and her close proximity to that child furthers the mother/child bond and aids in both the mental and physical development of the child. Yet feminism wishes to speed the separation of mother from child in order to hasten the female's return to the workplace so she can do battle with the male in a futile attempt to better the male on his own ground.

Bear in mind that in the early development of Western civilisation right up to before the industrial revolution, the mother would remain in the home with the child and be responsible for the child's tuition and personal development up to a fairly advanced age. The bond between mother and child would be far stronger because of this and as such the mental development of the child would be far more advanced and as a result the child's superego would be more likely to develop to a greater degree.

The loving mother set a standard that was then passed down from generation to generation. Her daughters saw the example she set and she became their role model. Just as the strong and dominant father figure provided a role model to his sons, the loving and motherly female provided a role model to her daughters. The young females saw the strength, love and the critical role the mother played within the family and sought to emulate that. The natural and learned urges of the young female were to emulate their own mother and to have children and to raise those children in the manner similar to their own upbringing.

But just as tradition is taught and remembered, it can also be forgotten. As the feminist pushes for the woman do battle with the male and thus abandon her family for the workplace, the young females see this and seek to emulate the actions of their mother. Just as young people who are without a father figure lack discipline and order and risk becoming tearaways, young females and young males are both affected by the lack of a loving motherly figure as this stunts a child's early mental development.

The female's hardened attitude to the male that now sees her view him as the enemy, and not the lover, protector and partner, also rubs off on the next generation. Rather than seeing the male as the other part of the complementary pair, the female sees the male as someone she should compete with – this is highly unnatural. Imagine back in the early days of Western society if the male and female had competed with one another and not worked together, Western man would never have survived. Remember, males and females working together and forming family units is the foundation of Western society. To break up the nuclear family by either removing the father or the mother is to tear apart the very foundations of the West.

For young females to be brought up by hardened, unnatural and unloving mothers that prioritise their career over the good of their children is to attack the very foundation of Western society and to undermine not only the development of the next generation but also the development of all future generations thereafter. But that is exactly what those behind feminism wish for. Feminism can be classified as an unnatural ideology – one based in self-aggrandisement that prompts the female to throw off her natural role as a mother and loving partner in order to 'achieve' on an individual level and in a way that is not conducive to the growth and maintenance of Western society.

The loving mother was not just a homemaker and was certainly not a 'slave' to her male companion as the feminist would like us to believe. The loving mother was the beating heart of the home and was crucial to the mental development of the next generation of the family. By providing stability, love and constant care and attention she nurtured mentally balanced children that would be more likely to accept and learn the morals and values that make up a developed superego.

By ensuring the child was in the right mental state to be able to learn, grow and develop into being a productive and balanced member of society, the mother played a crucial role in the development of Western civilisation. Was the role of the mother as the caregiver more important than the role of the father, or was the role of the father as a disciplinarian more important than the role of the mother? The answer, much to the annoyance of the feminist, is that both were and still are equally important.

To develop a cohesive society, the people who make up that society need to be mentally balanced and highly developed. The more highly developed and mentally balanced individuals are, the more developed their superego can be, and with a higher superego comes a higher level of moral reasoning. These high moral values and shared traditions are what bind homogenous groups of people together into communities.

It can thus be held that the Western female is the mother of Western civilisation as she nurtures the young and helps them develop through constant care and attention. The Western female played a pivotal role in the development of the next generation and helped the next generation develop a higher form of consciousness that served to bind Western society together.

The Western female was never less important than her male counterpart, nor was it intended for her to compete with him. The male and female were designed to complement one another and to come together to form a pair that held a value that was more than the sum of its parts. It follows that feminism is an attack not just on the male, but also the female and the whole of Western society as it seeks to undermine the beating heart of Western civilisation – the loving mother.

10
THE ROLE OF FEMINISM – THE DESTRUCTION OF THE FAMILY UNIT

The nuclear family is the cornerstone of Western society; it is central to the Western way of life. The family bond originated out of evolutionary pressure; Western man was forced into lasting partnerships in order to both defend and raise his children. Individuals who decided to give up on their partners inevitably saw their offspring perish and their genetic lines erased, however those couples who stuck together and worked as a family unit to ensure the survival of their offspring saw their children survive and mature and their genetic line carried on.

The coming together of man and woman was then enshrined in religious and state law. As individuals grouped together as tribes and tribes became nations, state and religious law sought to sanctify marriage and set the couple and the nuclear family above all else – a bond for life and one that should not be broken lightly. The importance of this family unit has been discussed extensively in the context of the significance of a two-parent family and the effect of both a mother and father being present when raising children.

We have discussed the importance of the strong father and the loving mother in the upbringing of children and how a two-parent family is crucial to the successful mental development of the child and most importantly in imparting the superego to the next generation. We have also discussed how in the West, the once strong family unit is now under attack, how divorce is on the rise and how children are increasingly being brought up in single parent homes. The effect of the loss of a strong father figure and disciplinarian in the home is quite clear to see.

It has also been discussed that the weakening of the superego has allowed the id to run free which has led to a rise in the number of divorces as both men and women choose to shirk the moral duties of bringing up their children as a couple, instead choosing to pursue a selfish path of individualism and pleasure. Along with the drive for individualism and pleasure, the enemies of the West have also mounted other attacks on the family unit, one of them being feminism.

Feminism operates under the guise of equality – that man and woman should be equal, when in fact men and women are not equal but different. Men and women make up a complementary pair and when together form a unit that is more than the sum of its parts. A happy home is supported by both a mother and a father, but the input of the father and the input of the mother are both markedly different, yet equally important.

Feminism sets up a dichotomy where men and women are natural enemies – it attacks the natural order of society and seeks to create a war between the sexes. Feminists seek to create a false battle where women need to overcome and dominate the males around them. Feminism is not a progressive movement that seeks to free women, but a divisive ideology that wishes to separate men and women from their natural roles as partners and instead seeks to set them against one another.

Make no mistake, feminism is an ideology of hate – hate for natural, strong masculine males, but also hate for the natural loving and feminine female. It is an ideology that seeks not equality, but for the female to dominate the male on his own grounds. It is an ideology that wishes to transform the female from being a natural, loving and compassionate individual into little more than a poor substitute for a man. Feminism seeks to break down natural boundaries and turn natural gender roles on their head. However these natural boundaries and gender roles are some of the founding blocks that served to build Western civilisation.

The drive for feminism within the West has had profound effects – not only does it lead to the death of the loving mother, but it also increasingly leads to the destruction of the family unit. How can man and woman come together as a complementary pair, as lovers, friends and partners, when they are being set against each other as if they were natural enemies? The whole overarching thought process behind feminism sets men up as the natural enemy and oppressor of the female – and who in their right mind would choose to settle and form a lifelong bond with their enemy and oppressor?

The whole basis of modern feminism is built around one central belief – that society is one big 'patriarchy' – a social system where men have the upper hand and control the running of society, to the detriment of females who are subservient to the authority of the male, and are in effect little more than slaves to their male counterparts.

In the feminist's thought process it logically follows that if the woman is oppressed by the male, if she is nothing more than his slave and marriage is just a way of state and religious law ratifying that slavery for life, then women should reject marriage.

Following this rather radical line of thought is the even more extreme idea that we live in a world where 'rape culture' is prevalent. In feminist theory, rape culture is a concept in which rape is pervasive and normalised in the West due to societal attitudes about gender and sexuality. In essence, rape culture is the bizarre theory that all men are potential rapists and rape is something men see as healthy. The theory of rape culture also states that men use rape as a tool to exert control and power over females within society.

This bizarre set of beliefs would be laughable – if they weren't so dangerous and weren't influencing the minds of so many young women in Western society. Once young women buy into this warped theory, it is little or no wonder that the family unit becomes the first and most obvious casualty. The notion that women are essentially slaves to men, held in servitude by the threat of rape no less, is hardly a notion that is going to endear women to men.

Now extrapolate that idea – women are told that they are slaves and they live under the constant threat of rape which is used as a tool to control them by their slave masters. Their slave masters are of course men who are all part of an overarching patriarchy that seeks to exert control over all women. How could any woman who believes this nonsense ever engage in a healthy, trusting and loving relationship with a man?

This very notion is one that could not be more divisive to the family unit. The coming together of man and woman is vital to the survival of any racial or cultural group – but if the men and women who made up a particular group were set against one another and made to resent each other the chances of that group surviving would diminish rapidly. Those who are propagating these feminist ideals are propagating an attack on Western society which is wholly destructive and divisive – they are literally attacking the cornerstone of Western civilisation by setting the two constituent parts of the family unit against one another.

Before these points are advanced any further, let us take a close look at the underlying thought process and 'facts' behind terms like 'patriarchy' and 'rape culture'. Firstly, it goes without saying that men do hold a disproportionate power in the structures that have emerged and developed in Western society – however it does not follow that such power is either oppressive nor does it follow that men are more important or that men exist on a higher level than females.

Males do take leadership roles within society more readily than females – however that is because the male is naturally the disciplinarian who imparts order, a trait important to any successful leader. This of course does not make the female obsolete or less important than her male counterpart as feminists would like to claim. The role of the female is that of a loving mother and partner who nurtures, cares for and oversees the early mental development and growth of her children. The future of any society or nation lies within its youth and what role could be more important to a well-functioning society than ensuring the development of the next generation?

The female's role is not solely in childrearing; the female also plays an important role in supporting her male counterpart. This support and love is something that allows men to achieve more than they could on their own and in turn allows greater advancements within society – as such it is commonly said that behind every great man is a strong woman. Whilst men who enjoy the support and love of a good woman are more likely to emerge as authority figures and take leadership roles in society, men also serve as protectors and guardians to the females who support them. Support is not a one-way street and men and women have always supported each other in different ways as they both complement one another.

The feminist however does not acknowledge this. The feminist wishes to create a conflict between man and woman, with the male being painted as the oppressive slave master who wishes to keep the female down and the female being presented as the oppressed victim who needs to break free and regain her independence. But under quite simple examination the idea that the male seeks to turn the female into a slave falls apart.

Crucially, no slave master would ever put their life before that of his slaves in order to protect what was mere property to him. Slaves are merely a commodity, something that is measured in monetary worth and can be used as a medium of exchange. No master loves his slaves; he works them to their limit and sees them simply as a tool in the same way he would see a piece of machinery.

Yet millions of Western men have given their lives wading through the mud of foreign fields and blood of their comrades and enemies as they fought to protect the lives and liberty of their wives and children. A man who is willing to give his life for another person must view that person in nothing but the highest regard – and the highest regard is what Western civilisation has always had for the Western female.

In times of war or hardship it would not be unreasonable to think that a slave master might put his slaves on the front line, to use them as cannon fodder and expend their lives to ensure his own safety. The Western male has never done this; when war has broken out the woman has always stayed at home, safe from the dangers and hardships of battle as the man has gone to fight in order to protect her liberty. But when did the slave master ever risk his life in order to protect the liberty of his slaves?

In times of disaster it was always women and children first – men would happily go down with the ship and give their own lives so that women and children would be afforded safety. It is doubtful any slave master would choose to fill the lifeboats with their slaves and go down with the ship to ensure the safety of their property above themselves.

The feminist however will eagerly tell you that staying in the home was never a luxury for the female and that the home certainly wasn't a safe space. The feminist will tell you that the homemaker was not free, nor did she have her liberty – the feminist will try to tell you that the home was a prison. The feminist will attempt to claim the homemaker was essentially tied to the home as a prisoner to a cage, whilst the man was free to go and work and carve out a lucrative career in the freedom of the outside world.

It is true that women did stay at home; they did look after the children and they did support their men as homemakers. But whilst women were at home, the men went out on fishing boats braving the wild seas; they went down mine shafts and risked being crushed to death or being asphyxiated by poison gas. Men also enlisted for military duty to protect their settlements from raiders and rival tribes – literally risking their lives on a daily basis.

The woman may well have stayed in the home and acted as a mother and homemaker – but she did not remain in the home as a slave who missed out on the wonders that her male counterpart enjoyed. The woman may rarely have risen to the level of tribal leader, but neither did she face death on a daily basis from simply doing her job, nor did she march to war to be hacked to pieces on a cold foreign field.

There is another crucial attribute of slaves – they are almost universally looked down upon. No one looks up to a slave; no one worships a slave and no one looks to a slave as a source of inspiration. Slaves are the lowest strata of any society and are held in low regard; something that the feminist will claim is true of women in Western society – however nothing could be further from the truth.

Women were never looked down on, but in fact women were deified in Western civilisation. One of the earliest classical writings,

Homer's *Iliad,* is an epic tale of the Trojan War and the exploits of the heroes who fought on both sides. One could get caught focusing on the battles, the male heroes or the immense scale of the war that encompassed the Greek states – but that would be to lose sight of the reason for the war, the love of a woman. Helen of Troy was the woman with the face that launched a thousand ships. Tens of thousands of men were fighting a war that engulfed ancient Greece, and it was all for the love of one perfect woman. One would find it hard to imagine a war being fought for the freedom of one lowly slave!

This deification of females and the female form is a theme that is present in Western literature, art, poetry and song. From the earliest Western texts the notion of beauty and the central role females played in society is always present. This is hardly the work or the actions of a civilisation that scorns females or treats them as slaves. Women were not beneath men, but often an inspiration to them and the very reason that men fought with such bravery and conviction and strived for such excellence.

Women were always looked up to in Western society – as mothers, wives and for their beauty and femininity. Western civilisation noted the differences between men and women and celebrated those differences; it did not pit one against the other, it did not compare the two and it did not cause the two to go into competition – but most importantly it never forced one to try to become the other.

With the term 'patriarchy' comes the even more troubling term 'rape culture'. Feminists will gladly tell you that every male is a potential rapist; this in itself is a flawed and ridiculous argument. The statement is actually factually true as indeed every man could potentially commit rape, just as every woman could potentially murder her own children. This is of course an absurd way to look at either men or women. Just because a small proportion of women smother their babies when suffering from postnatal depression, no man would go into a room and view every woman in that room as a potential child killer, and any woman who views every man as a potential rapist would be equally unreasonable.

However the unreasonable notion that every man should be viewed as a potential rapist is exactly the way in which feminists want women to view men. Feminism doesn't care for being reasonable – feminism intends to stoke hatred for men. The notion that every man is a potential rapist is a powerful tool in the feminist arsenal when it comes to promoting hatred and fear of men and causing further division between the sexes. What could be a more powerful tool in order to create hate and division between the sexes than to have every woman view every man as a potential threat to her safety?

Let's examine 'rape culture' further though and put the term under the microscope. Rape is surely one of the most heinous crimes and an act that no one should ever be subjected to. As such rape is an act that is looked down on by everyone in society. This is illustrated by the fact that when rapists are apprehended and imprisoned other criminals within the penal system attack them. The very dregs of society who have broken the law and need to be separated from society view rapists as subhuman vermin. That alone says an awful lot about the way sexual predators and rapists are viewed, and is hardly indicative of a society in which rape culture is prevalent.

The fact that rapists are outcasts even among criminals is a barometer of how poorly sex offenders are regarded. Bearing that in mind, the idea that there is a prevalent culture of rape amongst males, where males exert their power over females through sexual assault, is insane. But despite the theory of rape culture being utterly insane, it is still a powerful tool for the feminist as those who believe it learn to fear and hate the men they should love and embrace.

The urge for sex is a natural drive; it is governed by the id and is part of the pleasure principle. When a woman says 'no' to a male, the male's superego kicks in, his moral values and reasoning tell him that it is wrong to go forward with the sex act despite the cravings of the id which seeks to satisfy its lustful desires. The male's superego tells him it is wrong to force the female into having sex and hence he withdraws. That conscience for the feelings of the female is part of the developed psyche and is something that is imparted to the man during childhood by his mother. However there is also the fact that rapists are seen as the lowest of the low, hence those with a strong vision of an ideal self would never seek to carry out such a heinous crime. The ideal self is of course imparted to the man during childhood by his father and other male role models.

Western civilisation and the developed Western superego would never have tolerated rape or 'rape culture'. Rape is abhorrent and goes against the very natural urges of a man to protect, love and cherish women. Western man risked his life crawling through mine shafts and braving the open seas to provide for his wife and loved ones. Western man marched to war to protect his tribe and his family. Western man was not a slave master who used rape as a weapon, but a loving and caring partner who relied on his wife for love and support – and in return he loved and supported her.

The love and support that man and woman showed one another within Western Society was born through hardship and mutual cooperation. This mutual cooperation was necessary to ensure the survival of both the couple and their children. Men and women were never meant to be in competition with one another. Men and women were intended to be married to one another and to cooperate as a pair. By cooperating as a pair men and women could achieve more than they would have had they remained alone.

Feminism is an anti-family movement, a movement that attacks the very heart of Western culture. Feminism seeks to destroy the feminine beauty of the female and transform the woman into a more masculine creature so she can compete with her would-be partner in a pointless struggle for dominance. This war of the sexes is a wholly unnatural social construct manufactured by the enemies of the West. Feminism is another tool used by those who wish to destroy the West, and those who buy into it are being duped and used.

Feminism sets young women against men and builds distrust between the sexes. Feminism makes the man the 'enemy of the woman' in an effort to prevent loving bonds forming between the two. Feminism seeks to break the complementary pair that lies at the heart of Western life. Feminism is a tool that is used by those who wish to undermine Western civilisation as the feminist mindset undermines the formation of the family unit. Feminism also serves to increase the rate of divorce within society as married women buy into the nonsense that they need to break free from the chains of their slavery.

Women were never slaves to their men, but supporting and loving counterparts who in return for their support and love received love, safety and protection for both themselves and their children. There is no greater testament to this love and adoration than the fact that men would happily give their lives and go to their death in an orderly fashion with a smile on their face in order to ensure the safety of their wives and children.

Feminism seeks to undermine the cornerstone of Western society – the nuclear family. Feminism is an attack on the loving bonds and trust that act as a glue which bind the family unit together – as such feminism represents a threat to Western civilisation itself.

11

THE ROLE OF FEMINISM – THE REDUCTION OF THE WESTERN BIRTH RATE

Feminism is an attack on the West, a divisive ideology that seeks to turn women against men and break the natural loving bonds that exist between males and females. The complementary pairing of man and woman has served the West well and literally built Western civilisation through mutual support and the growth of the nuclear family.

Feminism does not only attack the male, but it also attacks the female. In order to allow the female to unnaturally compete with the male, and in order to achieve a sense of false equality, the female must alter her behaviour and adopt increasingly masculine traits. The female must lose her femininity, her loving, caring and nurturing side and must become hardened to her natural motherly and homely instincts. This represents the loss of one of the two components that is vital to the upbringing of a healthy and developed child – the loving mother.

Feminism also demonises the male. Feminism propagates lies of a 'patriarchy' and 'rape culture' in order to make women distrust and even hate men. These beliefs set up a false dichotomy of the male being the slave master and abuser and of the female being the slave and the victim. This ideology of hate turns the woman away from her natural partner, lover and friend and creates an air of distrust between women and men. Trust however is the obvious foundation of any loving relationship, so with distrust and hate and a growing manufactured and false battle between the sexes, the big casualty is lasting relationships, marriage and the nuclear family.

Women no longer want to be loving mothers, instead choosing to follow a path where they favour competing with males in the workplace rather than having children. It is not enough that women increasingly want to compete with males and become like males – thus having less children, but it is now a sad fact that women see children as a barrier to achieving their goals and see motherhood as wholly undesirable and something that holds them back.

For the feminist, being a mother is not an honourable pursuit – it simply makes the woman a slave to her male counterpart and ties her to him. Children are no longer desirable; they are a drain on time, resources and money. Children have gone from being a natural and fulfilling addition to a woman's life to being simply baggage that slows a woman down in her race to achieve material goals.

This is a key facet of the destruction of the Western soul and spirituality that the enemies of the West seek. The warm happiness and spiritual fulfilment that a loving couple gain from raising a family is replaced by individuals seeking greater material wealth. Material goals are put before everything, and the spiritual and soulful desires that brought loving couples together to procreate are now seen as a barrier to the new false idol to which Western people dedicate their life – materialism.

The rise of the notion that a child is no longer desirable and in fact holds a woman back has obviously affected the Western birth rate in a dramatic way. But it is not enough that women decide to simply not have children by avoiding loving relationships and marriage. Women now decide to kill their unborn children in order to forgo motherhood and continue down a path of personal gain and materialistic pursuits.

The West has witnessed the meteoric rise of abortion. We have talked earlier about the id and its selfish drive for pleasure and satisfaction and the superego and its drive for moral duty, values and selfless commitment to one's family and the larger community. Having a child and caring for and nurturing the next generation of one's people is the most selfless and noble act for a young woman to undertake.

Abortion is the most selfish and immoral act; to abort a healthy child – essentially to kill your unborn baby in an effort to ensure your own selfish and materialistic gain – is the single most unnatural thing a woman can do. The overwhelming natural instinct has always been for the parent to put the child first at any cost. The loving parent would always go without if need be in order to ensure that their offspring had everything it needed. The loving parent has always had an overwhelming drive to protect their child and keep their child safe – even if that meant the parent putting themselves at risk.

The developed superego and Western moral code always put the protection of the young first. Once an adult had brought a child into the world, the adult was no longer the centre of its own universe – the child was, and for the sake of that child the parent would strive relentlessly to ensure the child enjoyed the best quality of life possible.

The love for a child was once selfless and unconditional, now it is anything but. The love for oneself and materialistic gain is now so great that killing one's unborn baby is not only desirable, but it is socially acceptable. Every natural drive has been turned on its head. This is yet another victory for the id, as immediate selfish gain is prioritised above the long-term well-being of one's child and the responsibility one should have toward that child.

Obviously, there are of course cases where abortion should be considered by a woman, but these are few and far between. In the case of conception through rape or conception through incest where a father, brother or uncle is sleeping with a family member then of course abortion could well be justified – the same is true in underage relationships or where a minor has been groomed into sexual relations with an older male. There is also the case of children who will be born with major birth defects or significant disabilities which would drastically decrease the quality or length of life of the child. Finally, if the development of the child in some way puts the mother's life at risk and the continuation of the pregnancy or childbirth would likely result in the death of the infant and mother, it is best the infant is terminated.

However, make no mistake: to terminate the life of a healthy baby out of selfish desire for material gain goes against every natural instinct a woman should feel. Abortion effectively takes the natural and motherly instincts a woman should feel and turns them on their head. What's more, wide-scale abortion in the West effectively terminates the future of Western man. Every year in England and Wales alone there are over 180,000 abortions; factor in the rest of the UK and you will likely reach a figure of around a quarter of a million unborn children being killed every year in Britain alone.

What is even more frightening than the sheer number of abortions is the fact that the vast majority of those abortions are carried out on Western females and represent the deaths of hundreds of thousands of Western babies – something that will no doubt please the enemies of the West.

The feminist will claim it is the woman's right to choose, it is her body! But that is not strictly true; the body of the child is a separate human who is composed of the DNA of both the mother and father – it is a living, breathing baby with a heart and mind. What's more, from a very early stage of development the child feels pain and reacts to its environment.

Feminism sees abortion as a triumph of power and control for the female. Abortion is seen as a way for a woman to break free from the shackles of the 'patriarchy' and rebel against nature by throwing off her natural callings and truly advancing to a level where nothing can stop her in the pursuit of her new-found desire to compete with her male counterpart.

Abortion also represents the defeat of personal responsibility. It is yet another damaging and false moral code for the young Western mind, teaching the next generation that one should not have to take responsibility for one's actions and that taking the easy way out is morally acceptable. To make abortion socially acceptable emphasises that one can do as one pleases and pursue pleasure – in this case sexual pleasure – without having to worry about consequence or duty. Again, short-term gain and individual pleasure are put before responsibility and long-term commitment.

Feminism has further affected the birth rate by prompting women to see men as their competition, not their partners. The drive to compete with the male has made the man the enemy of the woman. This division between the sexes has led to women no longer wanting loving relationships as they distrust men and see them as the enemy. No one wishes to share a home and pursue a loving relationship with their natural enemy – but therein lays the problem, men and women were never meant to be enemies, and it is wholly unnatural for them to be so. Again the feminist mindset reduces the chance of women becoming mothers or having large families by setting the female against the male.

The final role of feminism is clear – it is not only an attack on femininity and the loving mother, it is not just an attack on men and the formation of couples and marriage – it is an attack on the very future of the West. The final goal of feminism, and the enemies of the West who promote it, is the reduction of the Western birth rate. Through warping the mind of Western females by the promotion of materialistic goals, promoting competition with, and distrust for, men and the growing trend of abortion on demand, the Western birth rate has been decimated.

The very future of Western man lies in mortal jeopardy as Western folk are no longer breeding and are no longer having large enough families. Western couples leave it ever later to have children and put off their duty to their community for the extension of short-term materialistic pleasure which they wish to carry on long into their thirties and forties.

It is true to say that the future of any race or culture lies within their women's wombs. No race, culture or tribe that has ever survived and prospered has done so with a declining birth rate or an aging population. The future of a people lies in its ability to pass on it genes and then its morals and values to the next generation and to ensure that the next generation survives, prospers and carries on down the path laid out by its forefathers. If the birth rate of a group falls and the next generation is continually smaller than the last, then regardless of all else, that group faces certain extinction.

Western civilisation took stock of this fact and that is why the moral code passed down from generation to generation was to protect and cherish the woman and the child. The learned moral code and a key part of the Western superego that was passed down from generation to generation was that women and children come first, and if necessary the man should lay down his life in order to protect and shelter the next generation and those who would raise them.

Men took the most dangerous jobs; men left the home to go and fight wars and men toiled in order to feed, clothe and protect their families. Part of the developed Western superego – the very collective consciousness of Western man – was to ensure the survival of the females in society in order to always allow for the population to rebound and the maximum number of children to be raised even if the male population declined through war or hardship.

To go back to our analogy of bees, many worker bees can perish, as can many drones, and the colony can still recover. However the loss of the queen would be catastrophic as she is the one who gives birth to the next generation – without her there is no next generation. It would not matter how hard the worker bees toiled, or how much pollen they collected or how well they defended the hive – it would all be for nothing, a futile act, if they were the last of their kind. Without the prospect of a future generation to carry on their legacy, all the hard work and all the sacrifice would be in vain as their DNA and their colony would vanish, relegating them to extinction.

The same is true for humans, and it is exactly why the females in Western society have always been protected – because they, like the queen bees, are the ones who literally carry the future of their community within them. Western society knew that often there would be great conflicts, war and cataclysms and in those times brave and worthy men would make the ultimate sacrifice, because as long as the females of breeding age and younger survived, that sacrifice would not be in vain.

To put this on a very simple mathematical level – if society is composed of a hundred females and ten males, in nine months' time there can be a hundred females, ten males and roughly a hundred children. If a society is composed of a hundred males and ten females, in nine months' time there can be a hundred males, ten females and around ten children. One society has the chance to grow rapidly and increase in number, and the other is likely to reduce in number and have demographic problems which will most likely lead to its extinction.

This is why females were protected and kept out of harm's way – not because of the evil patriarchy that wanted to keep them from greatness nor because they were slaves, but because the future of the Western man lay in their wombs. The crucial issue is the replacement of the population; a society can either grow or be sent into decline due to the number of children it produces from females of breeding age. When discussing the number of children being born in any society there is a crucial figure to bear in mind, this figure is known as the replacement rate.

The replacement rate is defined as the number of babies needed per female of breeding age in order to simply maintain the population at its current level. The figure of 2.1 is widely considered to be the "replacement rate" – the average number of births per woman that will maintain a group's current population level. Many Western birth rates have now fallen as low as 1.3. By Western birth rates we mean the birth rate of people who are of European heritage – not those of immigrant populations.

The birth rate of 1.3 is a critical low point and to demographers this number has a special mathematical importance. At a birth rate of as low as 1.3, a group's population would be cut in half in less than half a century, creating a falling-off-a-cliff effect from which it would be nearly impossible to recover. In less than fifty years the population would halve, and the downward spiral would be so severe that it would be almost impossible for that population to recover.

As the birth rate falls, not only does the population decline, but there is also a demographic shift from a young population to an aging population. The aging population is no longer productive or reproductive and needs to be supported by the decreasing number of young people within that society. This demographic shift puts a greater pressure on the young, as rather than having time to procreate and raise families, they spend increasing amounts of time tending to the elderly.

This drive to protect the elderly and support the elderly results in longer working hours, more duties in the home and reduced free time which all hamper not only the time spent meeting prospective partners and making children, but also the free time available to raise children.

But the birth rate of Western women is only the tip of the iceberg. If we lived in a perfect society, which as discussed earlier is both homogenous and monocultural, a falling birth rate would still be a serious cause for concern as it would be an indicator that serious issues were plaguing the population and driving people away from the natural call to procreate and raise families. However, despite the issue of a declining population, the group would remain homogenous and be more likely to retain its culture and hence more likely to make the difficult recovery necessary in order to raise its birth rate and recover.

Monocultural societies have suffered declining birth rates during times of war, famine and hardship – however they have recovered afterwards. The birth rate sharply declined in periods of war where men were away from home fighting overseas and were separated from their wives. These periods were always followed by a 'baby boom' when the conflict was concluded as the men returned home and there was a natural drive to have children and repopulate.

Sadly we do not live in a perfect society – we live in an imperfect society. Western countries are now no longer monocultural, but they are multicultural and multiracial. Many different groups live within one wider society and as discussed in earlier chapters, these groups all have their own respective cultures, traditions and moral values that cause them to be distinct and to pull in different and sometimes opposite directions to the other groups within that wider society.

Earlier it was stated that if one group within a wider multicultural or multiracial society was to start to decline and shrink in number and lose its cultural ties which bound the individuals in that group together, it would likely be dominated, destroyed and absorbed by the other stronger groups within that wider society and hence cease to exist.

Western man now struggles with a critically low birth rate, and we know that the native populations of Western countries are in decline. However it is constantly stated that Western nations have a growing population – in fact the UK population has steadily grown over the last fifty years from 50 million to over 64 million. It is worth noting that 64 million is the official number which relies on official census data – this figure takes no account of those living within the UK illegally or those not filling out the census accurately – the likely truth is that the population of the UK is far closer to 70 million.

If those who are native to the UK are in decline, if their birth rate is falling, then there can only be one conclusion to why the overall population is increasing at such a rate – immigration and the rapid growth and explosive birth rates of the immigrant communities that have settled in the UK. This is a recipe for disaster for Western civilisation and Western culture, as due to the demographic issues plaguing Western nations, it looks increasingly likely that Western man will become a minority in his own homelands.

Western nations face a double-edged demographic sword – a critically low birth rate mixed with an explosive growth in the immigrant population, an immigrant population that is culturally foreign and often seeks cultural and social dominance over the native people. Dominance is a goal that is far more easily achieved when numbers and demographics are on your side – and those numbers and demographics are not in the favour of Western man.

Feminism has had several wide-ranging effects on Western society – it has driven a wedge between the natural partnership of man and woman, setting them against one another, it has changed the mindset of the female and made her more materialistic and most crucially it has caused a shift away from childbirth and reproduction that has drastically affected the Western birth rate. The enemies of the West and the individuals who push the feminist agenda know this, and they know what effect these trends will have on the long-term stability of Western society and the survival prospects of Western man.

Feminism is just one of the attacks on the Western consciousness that seeks to undermine the family and reduce the Western birth rate, but arguably it is the most important. Materialism and selfishness from both sexes have seen a huge rise in the number of individuals who choose not to have children, or who choose to have fewer children.

The defining characteristic of feminism that sets it apart from other attacks on Western man is that feminism seeks to actively break the woman's maternal instinct. Feminism seeks to repress every natural and motherly instinct a woman may have, ensuring that those who hold the future of Western man in their wombs are no longer willing to have children. Regardless of the number of men who would wish for a child, it is all but irrelevant if the females within the group refuse to play their part and choose instead to turn their back on the ideals of family and motherhood.

The West is now reaching a crucial point its history, a critically low birth rate is coupled with a large, growing and culturally aggressive immigrant community. If this continues, Western man will slowly disappear with a whimper rather than a roar and Western civilisation will be confined to the history books.

The Western female must regain her sense of selflessness and rediscover her natural feminine urges and motherly callings and join with the Western male to form the family bonds that served the West so well and helped lay the founding blocks for Western civilisation. If she does not, Western man will stand alongside the dinosaurs as a once great but now extinct form of life – but this is of course just what the enemies of the West and those who propagate feminism would wish.

12
WITHERING MASCULINITY AND THE FEMINISED MALE

As feminism has warped the Western female, turning her from a kind, caring, feminine and motherly woman into a shallow and selfish individual who wishes to emulate her male counterpart, the Western male has undergone his own transformation. The Western male, once the 'alpha', the strong father figure who dispensed order and discipline and was a beacon of authority, has become weak and feminised.

In a sickening and highly unnatural role reversal, Western man has shed his dominant, strong and manly ways and become feminised, weak and subservient. The strong hunter gatherer, provider, protector and guardian has withered, becoming emotionally driven and unstable due to a mixture of lamentable role models, a weakened role in society and an increasingly purposeless existence.

In his new role, the Western male adopts everything his forefathers would have once scorned. He becomes reclusive from other males, he dresses and presents himself in ways that are more akin to that of a female and finds himself increasingly unable to live up to his natural role as the 'alpha'. There are many reasons why the Western male has declined in such a way and they are a direct product of the sustained attack on the Western superego.

The enemies of the West have sought to undermine both the family unit and its individual constituent parts – the male and female. The enemies of the West have sought to subvert the natural order of life by reversing the role of the male and female – something that has weakened the West.

The breakdown of the family unit is the first and most obvious cause of the emasculation of males within Western society. The family unit is the cornerstone of Western society and a fully functional family unit is composed of a loving mother and strong father figure. Both the mother and the father have important roles in the development of a young child and both serve as role models to the child in different ways.

In early infancy both children spend nearly their entire waking day with their mother. This early part of human development is where 'attachment' takes place and the close bond between mother and child speeds the mental and physical development of the child. Children who have a stronger bond with their mother through their early development become more mentally advanced.

As time goes by and the child grows up, the amount of time the child spends with its mother will change. Young females will tend to continue to spend more time with their mothers, whilst young males would typically spend more time with their fathers. This helps the child to develop their natural gender roles.

As the authority figure and disciplinarian in the family, the father would have a crucial role in imparting the superego – the learned part of the psyche – to his son. An upstanding and strong father becomes an important role model to his son and helps the young male form an image of his 'ideal self' which as the young man grows and develops he strives toward.

The Western family unit has been under repeated attack from the likes of feminism, a relaxation in social attitudes toward both marriage and single parent families, and through a relaxation of the laws surrounding divorce. It is now more and more common to see single parent families where a father figure is not present in the household. This removes the disciplinarian from the home and leaves young males without a strong father figure who would serve as their primary male role model and source of inspiration for their ideal self.

The young male would naturally spend more and more time with his father as he grew up, developing his masculinity and learning how to become a man. In a world where there are an increasing number of broken homes, resulting in an increasing number of children who lack contact with their fathers, many young males now grow up without the influence of their father. In essence, this strips the young male of his primary male role model.

This leaves young males looking to their mother as their primary role model in the home, something that leaves the male feminised and emasculated. Despite there being good mothers who do their best to raise a family on their own, there is really no substitute for the discipline and order of a strong father figure – just as in infancy there is no substitute for a loving mother who an infant attaches to. Just as depriving a young infant of its mother causes stunted mental development and even depression in a small child, depriving young males of a father figure as they develop can have similar mental effects.

The young male who lacks a father in the home is increasingly likely to base his vision of an ideal self on his mother and hence more likely to adopt feminine traits. Whilst it is obviously a good thing that young females base their ideal self on their mother, for a young male this is not ideal as it prevents him from developing his natural gender role. Whilst the young male will learn compassion and empathy from his mother, his superego will not fully develop in the way a male's should and he will be unlikely to learn masculine traits and therefore in later life be unlikely to assume the role of a disciplinarian and authority figure.

Sadly, the problem of the single parent family doesn't exist as an isolated issue within an otherwise healthy and moral society. Society once had safeguards in place – community leaders and role models who could take on the role of a father figure for young males that came from broken homes. However this is less and less the case in the modern world.

The lack of a father in the home is now compounded by the lack of strong male role models within the community and a reduction in manly outdoor pursuits for young males to engage in. As discussed earlier, the scouting movement, the cadets and other strong male dominated groups that took young men out into nature and taught them how to be men have slowly been undermined and mothballed. Instead of working and competing alongside other males and learning from older, stronger males in the community, young men are increasingly confined to the home where they spend long periods in isolation playing computer games, watching television and reading comic books.

As social creatures human beings are used to working in groups and learning from personal interactions with one another. For young men, being outside in a group surrounded by other young men, roughhousing, fighting and competing against each other – as well as working together, learning from one another and forming bonds as friends – are all important social interactions. The young male learns from this group dynamic as different males strive to be the alpha and each young man learns his place in the group.

This group development is vitally important and it is lost when youngsters are confined to their bedroom engaged in solitary pursuits. It is noted that in today's connected world young people are not truly alone as they are connected to each other via mobile devices, computers, game consoles and tablets. However this virtual connection is not the same as proper human interaction as it lacks important characteristics present in face-to-face interactions such as eye contact and the ability to read another person's facial expressions. In these solitary pursuits group dynamics are rarely developed fully and youngsters become withdrawn from the real world and unable to interact as they should when presented with real face-to-face social interactions.

It also can't be stressed enough how important being in the natural world is for young males. The natural world is beautiful, but also harsh and often unforgiving. Being outside and taking part in physical pursuits toughens the male and allows him to be in touch with his natural side, learning to deal with the elements, the environment and the challenges that environment presents to him. This is in direct contrast to the overly coddled environment where the spoilt and over indulged youth spends his time in warmth and comfort whilst immersed in a fantasy world on the screen in front of him.

When the young males do go outside, the coddling follows them. Every form of physical activity has been tampered with and in some way pacified in the name of health and safety. At one time building rope swings, climbing trees and diving into rivers was the norm for any healthy young boy. Now these pursuits are off limits for fear of a grazed knee or bruised arm. Even the pursuit of playing conkers is now accompanied with a pair of safety glasses!

The strong and outgoing nature that used to be common in young boys is now actively discouraged, but that very nature is what turned boys into strong and upstanding men. The brave young boy who was the first to try the rope swing was a hero amongst his pals, but now he would be admonished. The very message this imparts is one of weakness – a feminised message that robs young men of their natural urges and callings.

Boys used to strive to become men. It was every young boy's dream to be acknowledged by his elders and accepted as a man. This ancient rite of passage is present in almost every culture. When Western man's ancestors formed their first tribes on the frozen plains of northern Europe they formed hunting parties and braved the elements to bring food back to their dwellings. When the young males came of age they were taken out by the older established males who taught them the ways of the tribe. The younger males learned to hunt as part of a group and their skills were honed by the older, more experienced, males.

The younger males looked up to and admired the older males and their first hunt with the group was a rite of passage – the important juncture where the boy became a man. This passing down of masculinity helped the young male develop his superego by presenting him with role models that he looked up to and based his ideal self on.

The young male would feel immense pride and a sense of belonging when he was accepted into the adult group and became one of the mature males of the tribe. This sense of belonging and acceptance gave him a huge sense of self-worth and self-esteem and made him feel like he belonged. This sense of pride and self-worth increased the strength of his bond to his tribe and his people, and thus helped him develop into a man who wished to protect and serve his own people and ultimately become a father and pass down the skills and morals that were once passed down to him.

This trend of the son following the father and undergoing a rite of passage was something that continued throughout history right up until the West underwent deindustrialisation. When young men left school, they would often go to work in the traditional industry that was predominant in their town or city, and they would usually go to work with their father. These industries were strong and masculine industries that strengthened the male spirit and tested his body – mining, fishing, heavy industry and manufacturing. They were also industries that taught young men a skill or a trade, something that a young man could take pride in.

The young man would look up to his father and wish to follow in his footsteps, and when he left school and went to work at his father's place of work in the industry that had provided for generations of his family, the boy would become a man. The young apprentice would take pride in learning a trade. He would feel that he was making a worthy contribution to his community, and contributing financially to his family. Ultimately, this would allow him to move on and start his own family.

The young males were surrounded by older males who would teach them the skills they would need to hone in order for them to succeed in the workplace. These skilled males were in essence no different to the skilled hunters who led the hunting parties that welcomed the young men of the tribe when they came of age. The older males imparted skills to the young men and helped the young men build their superegos through the development of the ideal self. Just as thousands of years ago young men developed into adults and went on to teach future generations how to hunt, as time progressed young men became adults and taught future generations the skills they needed to succeed in the industry in which they worked.

Finally, when the young man had cut his teeth at work, he was welcomed into the community pub where he could relax and share a well-earned drink with the men he had once looked up to but now worked alongside. There was no divisive generation gap that separated father from son; the son wished to be like his father and carry on his family traditions. This way of passing down the family lineage from father to son was central to the Western superego and tied the current generation to the past and in doing so created strong masculine men.

With the decline of industry and the closure of Western manufacturing, many of the towns and cities built around those industries fell into ruin. Once proud men either languished on state benefits and sat at home drinking and smoking or were forced to 'retrain' in jobs they would have found humiliating and demeaning – both of these outcomes left many men feeling robbed of their pride. As the old industries declined, and working-class areas became sink estates, the local pubs closed and communities were left shattered.

No longer did young men go to work with their fathers and undergo a rite of passage and become a man. A huge generation gap emerged where a father could not relate to his son and the son never became a man in his father's eyes. The strong masculine male was an individual with purpose and pride, a man who would go on to be a strong father and impart discipline and order to his children. But when robbed of that purpose and pride the male became weak.

Young men watched their fathers waste away on the sofa, shadows of their former selves. Young men then adopted poisonous role models in lieu of their fathers and other strong males who would have shaped them in the workplace. The poor male role models presented to young men are very often weak, ineffectual and highly feminised males. As discussed earlier, these poor role models impart a defective superego to the young man searching for an image of an ideal self to work toward.

The rotten role models presented by the enemies of the West showcase everything that is wrong with society. These so-called role models emphasise the pursuit of selfish hedonistic pleasure, push notions of rebellion against the elders in society and make fun of tradition and culture. The role models placed in front of young men are no longer warriors, explorers, captains of industry or inventors – they are metrosexual mixed-up men who blur the lines between male and female.

Metrosexual men who own hair straighteners, wear make-up, dress in skinny jeans and spend hours in front of the mirror getting ready, do not build strong nations. That is not to say men shouldn't be well groomed and well presented. The well dressed, groomed and handsome man was the epitome of the Western male. Being well shaved, styling one's hair and wearing a sharp suit were something to be admired. But when men start wearing make-up, carrying handbags and dressing in clothes that are better suited to women, a line has been crossed and increasingly the Western male is now on the wrong side of that line.

Just as the enemies of the West placed hedonists and feminists in front of young women to turn them away from their natural motherly calling, the enemies of the West placed feminised males in front of young men to break the strong Western man.

We have discussed why strong males are important to Western society – they make good fathers, they build strong communities and they impart order and discipline which enables a strong superego to be imparted to the next generation. A strong shared superego helps a group to pass down their moral values and traditions from generation to generation – something that helps make a society cohesive, as a sense of shared heritage and tradition ties communities together and builds a strong culture.

A strong male is also important to the natural and healthy female. A healthy female chooses to mate with the 'fittest' male. The fittest male is not defined by the modern meaning of the word 'fit', which relates solely to physical attractiveness. The fittest male is the best provider; he is strong and dominant and is a male that a female can imagine having children with. The female chooses the fittest male on his ability to provide for her and her children and on his ability to act as a protector, guardian, lover, provider and strong father.

When a female chooses which partner she is to give herself to she is choosing a male with whom she seeks to form a lasting bond and raise children with. A female wouldn't choose a weak, sick or defective man, as that male would be unlikely to be able to give her everything she needed. Importantly, the female isn't looking for a man solely to provide for her own needs, but is looking for a man to provide for her unborn children. The Western female knew that through the harsh winters and the times of scarcity a strong male was needed to ensure her children survived. It was part of the Western female's motherly instinct to choose a strong male as a way of protecting her children.

The female also looked at a prospective male partner and assessed whether his characteristics were something she would like to see expressed in her children. A healthy and strong male would likely father healthy and strong children. This selection process, where a female chooses the strongest mate, is highly natural and can be seen throughout the animal kingdom. Never does the natural and healthy female choose the defective or weak male to sire children with.

These basic biological facts and evolutionary pressures are now working against Western man. As the Western male becomes weak and feminised, no longer presenting an image of strength and masculinity – healthy-minded Western females look elsewhere to find a mate. The enemies of the West know this and are all too quick to present the Western female with a 'better option' than the Western male. The future of Western man lies in the wombs of the Western female, but Western man has no future if the wombs of the Western female are occupied by the seed of a foreign people.

Western females who do search for a strong and dominant male are increasingly looking toward other cultures and other racial groups to find that strong male. Other cultures who have not abandoned their traditions and ways of life become a false beacon of hope to these lost Western females who seek a strong alpha male that will provide for them and protect their children. Of course, this only serves to further decrease the Western birth rate and further seal the fate of Western man.

What's more, as men from other cultures see the decline of the Western male, they increasingly target Western females as easy pickings. These men know the Western female will not be satisfied by the weak emasculated Western male and she will be instead attracted by the strength of a more dominant male that is part of a culture that is healthy and strong. So whilst feminists turn their backs on Western males out of a misguided hatred for men, those Western females who are still in tune with their natural instinct to find the fittest male also turn their backs on the Western male and choose to embrace foreign cultures in order to find a partner.

With a lack of a strong father, a lack of strong male role models in the community and a tendency to hide indoors and shy away from social interactions with other youngsters, young Western males have become weak. Instead of being outdoors in a natural and healthy environment learning the rules of life and forming bonds with both nature and their peers, increasingly young boys hide away in their bedrooms playing out fantasies in a coddled and over sanitised environment.

The feminisation of the Western male now starts from a young age and the destruction of purposeful and fulfilling employment and traditional rites of passage have ensured that the boy rarely becomes a man. Poor role models and a media that is intent on pushing the metrosexual male image further cement this feminisation process, imparting a warped vision of an ideal self upon young men that increasingly embrace traditionally feminine pursuits and who choose to present themselves and dress in an increasingly feminine manner.

The reasons for the feminisation of the male are all too clear. A feminised male will never make a strong disciplinarian or authority figure and presents a weakened image of the West to men of other cultures. Western women who still have their natural instincts intact turn away from these weak Western males. Instead they seek solace in the arms of strong men from other more dominant cultures, further accelerating the falling Western birth rate.

The enemies of the West fear the strong Western male; that is why they are hell-bent on attacking the structures and ways of life that make the Western male strong. The feminised Western male is not the same man who created Western civilisation. Strong men create civilisations, and it takes strong men to defend them.

13
THE DESTRUCTION OF LOVING RELATIONSHIPS

The two most natural instincts any creature possesses are the will to survive and the wish to reproduce. People often ask; 'what is the meaning of life?' Fundamentally the meaning of life is life itself – and that truth is expressed in the will of an individual to both survive and procreate. In the simplest terms, a successful organism attempts to prolong its own life for as long as possible and during that life seeks to reproduce and ensure its offspring survives to maturity.

Throughout the history of this planet the strongest, the best adapted to survive and those with a natural advantage over others have lived longer. The longer an organism lives, the more chances it will have to procreate and pass on its genes to the next generation ensuring that ultimately the organism lives on after death through future generations of its offspring.

This has led to natural selection and the slow improvement of the gene pool over time. The weaker individuals in any group died more readily and at a younger age, hence they were less likely to pass on their genetic code and the weaknesses within it. The strong survived longer and were more likely to pass on their genetic material. Hence, over time, weak traits and characteristics were likely to be bred out of a group and strong traits and characteristics were likely to become more prevalent within the group and over time those traits would improve further and become progressively stronger.

Over tens of thousands of years this slow and arduous process has led to many incremental changes and improvements and Western man has changed and developed to become what he is today. Two of the most unique traits of Western man are his ability to reason and his inventive spirit. These traits are surely a consequence of living in such harsh conditions during Western man's early development in Northern Europe.

If early Western man was not hard-working, tenacious and inventive he would have perished in the harsh winters as he would have either frozen or run out of food and starved to death. These conditions meant only the best managed to survive and went on to pass down their genetics which in turn improved the gene pool – this was the very beginning of Western civilisation. This same inventive and creative edge went on to give the world electricity, the combustion engine, great works of architecture as well as artistic and cultural masterpieces.

For all this to take place though, sex was necessary. Sex is a natural drive governed by the id. As such sex is something that we seek immediate animalistic satisfaction from. The fact that sex feels good and is so enjoyable is of course an evolutionary advantage. The survival of any organism depends on its ability to reproduce and if the act of copulation was painful, disgusting or undesirable that would be a major evolutionary flaw as the organism in question would be less likely to reproduce. Sex being pleasurable is an evolutionary advantage as it makes us want to do it; it tempts us into sharing our genetics and creating the next generation – hence ensuring our continued survival.

Early Western man soon learned not to be driven simply by sexual desire. As sexual desire is a product of the id, it needs to be restrained and controlled by a developed superego. This superego and mental control over sexual urges started to develop back in the earliest days of Western man's development.

We have already discussed the pressures on early Western man that helped create the beginnings of the nuclear family. Western man had the urge for sexual gratification, but because of the harsh winters and difficult conditions in Western man's northern homelands, a man that abandoned his partner was unlikely to see his offspring survive. The Western male had to stand by his female companion and they had to work together in order to protect and nurture their children and ensure their survival.

Those who gave into their primitive drives and pursued sex with many different partners, choosing to abandon their children, rapidly saw their bloodlines die out. Those who stuck with one partner and controlled their urges, confining themselves to sexual activity with that partner, saw their offspring survive as they were there to protect and nurture those offspring as part of a two-parent family. This was the beginning of the trend toward monogamy and lasting life partnerships.

At this point it serves us to be reminded that human beings, whilst still being a part of the animal kingdom, are much more mentally developed than other creatures. As such, the bonds we form with our life partners are based on more than simple attraction, sexual chemistry and the desire to procreate. Humans developed a powerful emotion which served to bond two individuals to one another for life – that emotion is love.

Love is the deeper emotion that causes a human to commit completely and exclusively to one single partner. Love binds us to our partner for life and provides powerful urges to cherish and protect our partner at all costs. Love is a crucial part of the superego and forms part of our conscience; it is something that allows us to bond with others on a higher level and most importantly it overrides the id – we forgo sexual pleasures with others in order to protect the feelings of the one we love. The fact we choose to stay loyal to one individual shows restraint and conscience which is indicative of a developed superego.

Love is the emotion that sets one person above all others in the eyes of their partner. It is the emotion that stops an individual straying and simply going off and pursuing endless sexual liaisons with random partners. Crucially, love transforms sex from an animalistic act based on self-gratification and pleasure alone into a loving act which satisfies the spirit as much as it does the body. Love takes sex to a higher level and thus promotes monogamy and lasting human relationships. Love builds the nuclear family and is thus responsible for helping to build Western civilisation.

As Western society developed, love was enshrined and ratified in the act of marriage. This is evidenced in modern marriage vows; '...to have and to hold from this day forward, for better or for worse, for richer, for poorer, in sickness and in health, to love and to cherish; from this day forward until death do us part'. The words 'love', 'cherish', and 'until death do us part', underpin every marriage. They are not a social or religious construct, but reflect a natural urge which religions sought to enshrine in law for the good of society.

This is another example of how religion and the state enacted laws around natural Western callings and sought to further strengthen and ratify the structures Western man had evolved in order to strengthen Western society. In a very real sense marriage is the ratification of nature's calling – a two-parent family bonded by love for life.

Marriage made it socially unacceptable to stray from one's partner. Marriage enshrined the loving couple, and the very concept of being spiritually bound to a single partner for life became part of the Western superego. Western man's collective consciousness and thus society as a whole frowned on those who gave in to their carnal desires and looked up to and praised those who prospered as clean living monogamous couples.

Those who chose to break the code of marriage, those who chose a life of promiscuity and gave into their id, were scorned by society. Men and women who had many sexual partners were looked down on and seen as dirty; as a result they were shunned by society. But it was not just society that punished the sexually promiscuous – nature did also. Those who had many partners and slept around were more likely to contract sexually transmitted diseases which reduced their capacity to reproduce and even shortened their lifespan. Both society and the natural world applied pressure on Western man in order to promote a monogamous lifestyle, those failing to live a monogamous life were punished either by the collective consciousness or by nature itself.

Imagine the effect it would have on Western society if natural and loving monogamous relationships were undermined. Imagine if sex became just a carnal desire and was divorced from love and emotion. Imagine if everything in Western society was sexualised in order to tempt individuals into giving in to their id, whilst at the same time the superego was undermined in an effort to create a society where wild promiscuous sex was the acceptable norm. This would undermine marriage, social cohesiveness and most importantly lasting monogamous relationships and the heart of Western society – the nuclear family.

But you do not have to imagine this scenario – the enemies of the West are doing just this. Through the constant sexualisation of literally everything we view and interact with and the relentless pushing of pornography, nudity and sexually-charged material, the enemies of the West have undermined love and the loving relationship in an attempt to reduce Western man to a mere sexual beast who craves to fulfil the animalistic desires of the id. Central to this attack on society, and one of the greatest negative influences on both society and the individual, is pornography.

Pornography is one of the most destructive influences on the Western superego. Pornography is simply sex for the sake of sex, pure carnal desires being fulfilled in a soulless and often degrading and debased manner. Pornography does not have a conscience for monogamy; it is by its very nature promiscuous, and the more partners, and often the more people that are involved in the sex act, the better. Pornography fuels the id and undermines the superego; as such it is highly addictive.

The sex acts carried out in pornographic films are not natural and loving sex acts between monogamous partners – but are often brutal and unnatural. The women employed by the porn industry are more often than not extremely beautiful and the acts they partake in are extremely degrading, humiliating and in many cases unnatural. Pornography is not just an attack on the superego and the foundation of the loving relationship, but is a way in which the enemies of the West can revel in the degradation, objectification and humiliation of beautiful Western females.

The first thing that is noted about pornography is the number of sexual partners each individual has. The sex acts depicted in pornography are not between monogamous partners, but instead both men and women have dozens if not hundreds of sexual partners over their 'career'. This sexual variety is then seen as desirable by those who watch pornography. The idea that it is desirable to have one sexual partner who satisfies the every need of their lover is jettisoned for the notion that satisfaction comes from many different partners who all fulfil a different need and perform a different sexual role.

The next highly damaging influence associated with pornography comes from the way in which men and women have sex on camera. Sex evolved to be a loving act, not an act of violence or degradation. Yet in pornography sex is more often than not degrading and violent. Women are dragged around, sodomised and degraded in a way that would not make a female feel loved, but instead make her feel used and worthless. Often more than just two people are involved in these acts – making these sex acts the very opposite of a loving embrace. The effect of this is for men to see women not as loving partners, and sex not as a loving act, but to see women as objects to degrade and humiliate, and for sex to be violent and debased.

There is also no doubt that the enemies of the West who push this filth get some sick satisfaction from watching beautiful Western females being degraded and humiliated in violent sexual acts in which they are treated like pieces of meat. The females who star in these films are unloved, unvalued and ultimately are portrayed as nothing more than soulless sexual objects.

Finally, sex simply for the sake of sex is not fulfilling. Western man has evolved to be satisfied by natural and loving sex in which there exists a greater bond between the couple involved than simply physical attraction. Pornography removes that natural component of the sexual experience and thus is not truly fulfilling. Pornography becomes like a drug; it is addictive and the 'high' lasts a short while but never leads to lasting fulfilment, so it needs to be indulged in more and more often, and the nature of the material viewed often becomes more and more extreme as the viewer searches for new experiences.

As a drug addict becomes used to a drug, smaller and less potent doses have less of an effect over time causing the addict to seek out larger doses or stronger stimulants. The same happens to the porn addict – over time softer and more restrained images and scenes have less of an effect and the addict seeks out material that pushes the envelope of degeneracy even further.

This overexposure to sexual material drives perversion, and sick fetishes emerge, further warping the mind of those who indulge in such material. But the problem is everyone indulges in this whether they wish to or not as Western man is now surrounded by pornography and sexually explicit material. Pornography is no longer restricted to dirty back street stores and sweaty truck stops; sadly pornography is now part of the mainstream. 'Porn stars' are now seen as celebrities and held up as twisted role models and what would once have been seen as sexually explicit material is now shown on prime-time television.

All of this fuels the id and increases Western man's drive for sex and sexual release. Western man's collective consciousness and superego are further damaged as those within Western society look to fulfil their carnal desires as many times as possible with as many partners as possible rather than forming loving bonds with a single partner. The biggest victim of this drive to sexualise Western society is the nuclear family; again the cornerstone of Western civilisation is under attack.

But where are the feminists you ask? The feminists should surely be up in arms over pornography and marching on those who produce it! Pornography is sexually degrading and objectifies women, presenting them as mere pieces of meat that are simply there to satisfy male sexual desires. However the feminists are suspiciously silent. The same feminists who attack and picket beauty pageants are nowhere to be seen when it comes to opposing pornography.

Beauty pageants are however not sexual. Beauty pageants seek to hold up Western beauty as an ideal; they are part of the deification of the Western female. Beauty pageants hold up the natural and high ideal of a beautiful and feminine female as a role model and ideal self for young females. Feminism hates femininity and beauty as those are womanly virtues, virtues that the feminist seeks to supplant as they push for the female to become ever more masculine.

So whilst the feminist attacks the beauty pageant and scorns the noble practice of holding up natural beauty and worshipping true femininity, the feminist stays silent on the degrading practices and sexual violence of the porn industry. This is quite simply because both feminism and pornography are weapons used to destroy the West and attack the Western nuclear family. Those behind feminism and pornography are one and the same.

The level of sexualisation within society and the availability of sexually explicit material and pornography is frightening – it is a sure sign of the total moral decay of Western society. Sexualised images, sexual themes and an increasingly sexualised sense of attire stirs and arouses the animalistic urges of the id. The highly sexualised society would be bad enough if it were just adults that were exposed to it. Adults with healthy and developed superegos could withstand much of the bombardment of sexualised material as the moral values they held would keep their id in check.

However, the sexualisation of society is extended to young people and even children. More and more children are exposed to sexualised themes, sexualised role models, sexual acts depicted on television and in film and even hard-core pornography which is now readily available and easy to access for anyone with the most basic technological skills. This leads to the destruction of the child's innocence and the sexualisation of children. This has a hugely damaging effect on the developing superego and imparts the warped moral values of promiscuous and unnatural sex being healthy, normal and desirable.

Just take the following lyrics as an example of the sexually charged material children are exposed to – this comes from the chart topping song by Rhianna – an idol to millions of young girls and a global megastar who has sold over 200 million albums and singles.

147

Her song 'S&M' was a global mega hit and enjoyed huge radio play and massive exposure on television. The lyrics are as follows:

Cause I may be bad
But I'm perfectly good at it
Sex in the air
I don't care
I love the smell of it
Sticks and stones
May break my bones
But chains and whips
Excite me

Rihanna is a role model to young girls and 'S&M' is a song that millions of these impressionable and often pre-pubescent girls would have listened to and sang along to. The song is highly sexualised and its themes are bondage, sex and sadomasochism, yet it is a pop song aimed at youngsters.

The sexualisation of children teaches young boys that females are pieces of meat to be objectified and that to have as many partners as possible is a noble and healthy pursuit – it forces the male into thinking that females are not to be loved and cherished but are there simply as sex objects. The sexualisation of young girls teaches them that they should present themselves in a sexualised manner for the pleasure of young men and that sexual attention on an animal level should be desirable and sought after.

This leads to an utterly warped set of moral values that, when presented to children, damages the formation of their superego. Without a well-developed superego youngsters are left answering to the call of their id which leads them to pursue a path of selfish and destructive pleasure. What makes this even more damaging is that the drive to sexualise children does not occur in a society where there are healthy role models, parental figures and safeguards to steer children back in the right direction.

Young girls now dress akin to little strippers and young boys fantasise about sex at an ever younger age. It has become normal for sexual relations to start at a younger and younger age when those taking part in them are not mentally developed enough to either truly understand the consequences of their actions or to deal with those consequences should they occur.

Western civilisation was built on the healthy two-parent family where strong and mature adults raised children and imparted a healthy superego to those children. Yet when children are still learning, developing and having their superego imparted to them, they are not ready to have their own children. For children to become parents and attempt to raise their own children, when they themselves are not fully mentally developed, is a recipe for disaster. A child is not suited to overseeing the mental and social development of another human being, and for children to be placed in positions of parental responsibility is a further sign of a decaying society.

Mentally undeveloped children now seek unnatural sexual relations fuelled by their exposure to pornography and sexualised images presented by the media. These youngsters crave warped, unnatural and often degrading sexual encounters which take place without love or emotional value. These children do not care for the consequences of their actions and are not capable of dealing with those consequences if they occur. The sexualisation of Western youth is one of the most grotesque and damaging attacks on Western man and Western civilisation.

Healthy sexual relationships were once confined to the bedroom and took place between two consenting and loving adults that had made a commitment to be with one another. Sex has now been unleashed in a way not seen before and is no longer subject to any social confines – it is a no-holds-barred, anything goes free-for-all that affects every aspect of our daily lives as Western society has become hyper-sexualised.

The healthy, loving and natural sexual relations that evolved and developed within Western society are now thrown to one side and replaced by unnatural sex that seeks to only please the body with no concern for the heart, mind or soul. The superego that imparted the moral value that sex should be between two people who are in a loving and stable relationship has been undermined, and the id now reigns supreme as people clamour for ever more sexual gratification with as many partners as possible.

This not only undermines the family and puts at risk the moral fortitude of the next generation, but it also undermines our own sexual and mental health as we seek out increasingly depraved acts to fulfil an id that is never truly satisfied.

However the greatest casualty of this 'sexual revolution' is the young. Not only do the young suffer as the divorce rate rises and more and more single parent families are created through wild sexual encounters between individuals who rarely think of the consequences of their actions, but the young also suffer as their minds are warped due to exposure to highly sexualised content in the media, the increasing availability of pornography and other influences that the enemies of the West have foisted upon Western society.

The destruction of the loving and healthy sexual relationship undermines the very core of Western society. Humans are a higher form of being, and sex has evolved from an animalistic sexual act to a spiritual and loving coming together of two compatible individuals. Once love is removed from the sexual equation we are reduced back to the level of animals – and what more could the enemies of the West want than to see Western man reduced to the level of debased cattle?

14

THE LOSS OF THE WESTERN MIND

The enemies of the West have sought to undermine Western civilisation by attacking its very foundations. The same devious individuals have also worked to undermine the structures and safeguards that have been erected in order to protect and strengthen Western society. The aim of this wicked scheme is to destroy the Western superego – Western man's highly developed shared mental consciousness.

By breaking the Western superego the enemies of the West seek to erase Western culture and the traditions and moral values that have been passed down from generation to generation within Western society. Once the culture that binds Western man together as a group and allows those within Western society to relate to one another is dead, Western civilisation shall not long follow it and Western man will face extinction.

Western man faces losing his mind, body, soul and his once mighty Western heart. Each of these four components is an important part of what made Western man the indomitable titan he once was. In order to break the four components that made Western man such a titan, the enemies of the West had to devise a way of twisting Western man's mind in order to make Western man susceptible to ideas that would otherwise seem insane.

To convince a people to abandon their partners and families, to convince a people to abandon their communities and culture and to convince females to rebel against their male counterparts would undermine any society. Ultimately these attacks on the West are an attempt to break the Western superego, but such a group of concerted attacks had to be carefully planned and carefully executed. Crucially these attacks had to begin somewhere – but where?

The attack on Western society began with the attack on the Western mind. The first logical place to strike is the psyche, as once the mind is reduced in its capacity to reason and the hardened mental fortitude of a people is turned to jelly, those people can be convinced of anything. Enslaving people and manipulating them by force whilst keeping them in chains is difficult and requires huge amounts of manpower and resources. To enslave Western man by subjugating him physically and putting him in chains would be unthinkable.

Western man could not have been tamed or defeated by any other race or culture on the planet in a conventional and physical sense. But imagine a situation where the mind of Western man was slowly broken down over time and the chains placed upon him were not physical but mental – where the cage that held him was not one made of iron or steel but was an invisible and intangible form of mental bondage that controlled his mind.

What could be a more ideal form of slavery than one that does not require chains, guards and constant supervision, but instead the slave is kept in place by his own subservient mental state? But what would make this devious trick even more impressive is if the slave didn't even realise he was a slave and instead thought himself to be free. For a man to believe he was free when in fact he was actually enslaved would be the greatest trick ever pulled. The most powerful cage that can be placed around a man is the illusion that he is in fact free – for when a man believes he is free he would never seek to escape his cage or rebel against his captor.

What's more, once the mind is enslaved and has a reduced capacity for reason, then thoughts, ideas and notions can easily be implanted in the mind regardless of their merit. Once the mind has been lost the other constituent parts of Western man – the body, soul and heart – could be attacked with ease by means of simply implanting further negative thoughts in the enslaved and impressionable mind.

Western man did not lose his mind overnight; he wasn't subdued in days, weeks or even years. It took decades of careful manipulation and brainwashing for him to be subdued to the degree he is today. At first Western man's mind was not bombarded with damaging material – at first Western man was drip-fed mental poison and over time those drips became a flow and in greater time that flow became a torrent. The poison fed to Western man was a highly toxic message of false moral values fed to him by the mass media. Over decades the enemies of the West who control the media have manipulated everything Western man has seen, read and heard. The brainwashing process has been slow, but it has been stunningly effective.

The brainwashing Western man underwent was not administered in an overt way. People were not dragged out of their homes at night and forced into gulags where they were subjected to mental torture against their will. Western man was not chained to walls or tied to tables screaming in agony as his captors beat new ideas into him. Western man was brainwashed in the comfort of his own home, in fact he chose to turn on the device that imparted that brainwashing and he willingly gathered around it with his wife and family. Western man was not coerced; he was not bullied or beaten, and he went willingly to the re-education classes.

The mass media is firmly in the grasp of the enemies of the West. The film industry, the music industry, the broadcasting media and the press are all under the control of those who wish to see the West fall. These different arms of the media use their respective channels to poison the minds of the Western populace and constantly pump out a torrent of damaging material intent on poisoning the Western mind.

This is not a new phenomenon; it has not been something that has come about over the last five or ten years, but is a long-standing and developed attack that has been taking place for decades. What's more, this attack has accelerated as the media's power has increased due to technological advancements and the increasingly connected nature of the world.

The very earliest hit films that were churned out by the devious minds in Hollywood pushed a destructive agenda. First let us go back to 1955 and examine an early film that turned the head of Western man and introduced a rebellious role model to the mind of Western youth with the express intention of fostering a division between father and son and creating a generation gap. This film was *Rebel Without a Cause*.

The film portrayed a troubled young teenager who couldn't relate to his father and mother and didn't want to follow in their footsteps – instead he chose to rebel against society, society's authority figures and the established way of life. Yet crucially, the rebel was the one without a cause; the rebel didn't fight for noble or worthy reasons, it was simply rebellion for the sake of it. The rebel was not fighting against tyranny or an oppressive and cruel master – but was fighting against a just, fair and decent vision of society.

The film was set in an era when a strong and cohesive community, a stable two-parent home and a smooth running society were still more or less the norm. *Rebel Without a Cause* went against all these healthy Western pillars of strength with the portrayal of its main character (the titular rebel), Jim Stark, being an underage drunk who was disrespectful to authority figures and his parents. Jim Stark smoked cigarettes, raced cars, got into knife fights, and would storm out of his parent's house whenever he pleased.

This kind of behaviour was unheard of at the time – especially in the middle-class setting where the film took place. Jim Stark was not the typical teenager; he was a fantasy figure dreamt up in the minds of devious men who wished to create division within Western society. All of the traits that Jim Stark displayed went against every established ideal of the time – essentially showcasing exactly how a teen should not act. Teens at the time did not act in the way Jim Stark acted and the character was not a portrayal of an ideal or normal teen. So why make a film showing how not to act, how not to behave and portraying a negative role model to millions?

The movie became a sensation and the main character Jim Stark became a role model to millions of impressionable youngsters who wished to follow in his footsteps. This is just an early example of how the media influences young people and creates tension within society by fostering divisions that previously did not exist.

As we have already discussed at length, Western society places great importance on the role of the family unit and on the father being a strong disciplinarian and role model. But even as far back as 1955 the poison was being poured out by Hollywood and the family unit was being undermined by turning children against their parents and creating a generation gap. The generation gap was to ensure that different generations of Western society would not relate to each other.

The generation gap is not conducive to a well running society. A cohesive society passes down its morals, values and traditions from generation to generation – so to create a gap between those generations jeopardises the passing down of that vital information. The generation gap jeopardised the continuation of Western culture and damaged the Western superego that had been passed down over countless centuries.

Fast forward forty years and these damaging films were still being made. The year was 1995 and the film *Kids* was released. *Kids* is yet another film about youth rebellion. The film centred on a group of teens led by two friends Telly and Casper. The group are aged twelve years and up and are sexually active, shoplift, abuse drugs and go as far as to beat a man to death in a park.

Despite *Kids* being released forty years after Jim Stark caused a stir in cinemas, the message pushed by *Kids* is startlingly similar to the message pushed by *Rebel Without a Cause* – youth rebellion. The big difference between the two films is not their core message, but their tone and graphic nature; *Kids* dramatically showcases just how far the enemies of the West have been able to push back the barriers of what is acceptable within Western society. Had *Kids* been made and released in 1955 there would have been riots, but in 1995 the film's release only created mild controversy which probably only served to gain the film more publicity.

Rebel Without a Cause was not alone in pushing the message of rebellion and was accompanied by other similar films. *Rebel Without a Cause* was also accompanied by rock 'n' roll – a musical revolution that pushed similar and equally destructive themes to those being pumped out by Hollywood.

Earlier we talked about the destructive lyrics that are pushed by role models within the music industry and the message that those role models impart to young impressionable fans. We discussed the lyrics of a handful of very popular songs and what message those lyrics imparted to young impressionable listeners. But again, this trend is nothing new; it also began in the 50s with groups like Bill Haley and the Comets who had a hit with the song 'Rock Around the Clock'.

By today's standards 'Rock Around the Clock' seems pretty tame – but after close examination of the song's message, it is clear to see that the moral of the song is to party all night with little or no regard for the consequences. It is clear where modern music evolved from and where the roots of modern lyrics lie. Whilst 'Rock Around the Clock' seems like nothing compared to the filth pushed by Lady Gaga, both have to be seen in context. Whilst Bill Haley sang simply about 'rocking around the clock', Lady Gaga takes this message to the next level and sings of being so drunk she has lost her phone, her keys and about how she doesn't even know where she is – but her conclusion is to 'just dance'.

Lady Gaga does indeed go far further than Bill Haley and the Comets ever did, but at the core of both songs is the same message – party endlessly and pursue hedonism. The big difference between the two songs is simply how far the envelope of taste has been pushed and how explicit the message has become. What pushes the envelope in terms of taste and morality now would have been completely taboo or even unthinkable forty or fifty years ago. Equally, what pushed the envelope in the 1950s would be seen as tame or even laughable now.

Those who have attacked the mind of Western man have done so slowly and methodically. To draw a simple analogy, they have cooked the mind of Western man as one would boil a frog. If you were to throw a frog into a pot of boiling water it would jump out in a bid to escape its fate; if however you were to place the frog in the pot and slowly turn up the heat, it would sit smiling until it was boiled to death.

Had the mental assault on Western man begun with a torrent of obvious and outrageous degeneracy, then people would have been less likely to accept what was being pushed, so the assault on decency started slowly and increased over time. But if this point needs to be hammered home further, simply imagine taking a recording of Lady Gaga and her antics back to the 1950s and trying to explain to those living then that Lady Gaga would be the acceptable standard in the early 21st century.

Yet those who wish to see Western civilisation crumble would tell you that the process you are reading about is simply 'progress', indeed the message being pushed has progressed, but that progression is anything but positive. There is however one area where Western society does seem to carry on progressing – and that is in the sphere of technology. Sadly though, the enemies of the West have used this technology against Western man and Western man's own industrious and inventive nature has been turned against him.

One of the most influential and world changing inventions of the 20th century would speed the decline of the West exponentially. That invention was the television. The filth being produced to warp the Western mind was no longer confined to the big screen or the radio – but the poison was now being beamed into homes and mesmerising families who gathered around this new technological marvel. Of the shows broadcast none were more addictive nor more destructive than the soap opera – daily tales of 'ordinary' people's lives that always seemed to showcase the worst and most degenerate aspects of society and play them out as if they were the norm.

The main characteristics that define soap operas are an emphasis on family life, personal relationships, sexual dramas and emotional and moral conflicts – but critically soap operas also address social issues that occur within society. Week in, week out, soap operas are the most viewed programmes on television enthralling huge audiences who increasingly buy into the plots and characters as if those plots and characters were all real.

Now imagine if a show that placed an emphasis on family life always showcased the worst of family life – rather than showcasing cohesive families that got on with one another, the show centred on families that argued, families where the mother and father had extramarital affairs, families that stole from each other and families where the children sought to undermine their parents. This is exactly what the soap opera does; it is a series of intertwining stories that showcase negative drama that would be undesirable in any functioning family unit.

Over time the soap opera seeks to normalise negative behaviour and instil a sense of false reality in the viewer. The goal of the soap opera is to make the viewer believe that the families being portrayed on the screen are normal and that their behaviour is acceptable. These repeated messages slowly creep into the collective consciousness of those who sit glued to their televisions with the intention of altering the actions and behaviour of the viewer. Over time the viewer becomes used to seeing families fighting, couples cheating on one another and friction between individuals within a community. The viewer eventually sees such behaviour as normal and as a result begins to replicate this negative behaviour within their day-to-day life.

Soap operas also present other social issues in a light that serves the agenda of the enemies of the West. Whether it is the acceptance of abortion, divorce, homosexuality or the normalisation of the multicultural society – soap operas are always the first to broach these subjects. As with films, soap operas start pushing their message in a moderate fashion and then push the envelope further and further. In the 1960s *Coronation Street* (a prominent British soap opera) featured its first divorce and was the first prime-time show in the UK to depict a suicide, and in 1998 *Coronation Street* introduced its first transsexual character. The writers of these soaps continue to push the envelope further and further just as the writers in the film and music industries do.

Soap operas have been engineered to highlight and glorify social discord within the family unit and the community – they almost always focus on negative facets of society and promote gossip and dishonesty. Soap operas also have the additional role of pushing negative social issues upon an unwitting audience much in the same ways films do – they simply do so on a more regular and sustained basis. But what makes soap operas even more dangerous is that over time the lines between reality and fantasy have become increasingly blurred in the minds of the viewer.

When the *Coronation Street* character Deirdre Barlow was wrongfully imprisoned on the show as part of the plot, there was public outcry. Thousands signed petitions for her to be freed; people printed t-shirts calling for her release and one complete idiot even donated £5000 to a fund calling for her freedom. However the most gobsmacking moment came when the then Prime Minister Tony Blair weighed into the debate and demanded an enquiry into her conviction – this was then echoed by national newspapers that soon joined the campaign for her freedom.

This just shows the devastating mental effect that television and film have had on the Western mind. An increasing number of people cannot even differentiate between what is reality and what is fiction and these people actually see characters portrayed by actors and actresses as real-life people who face real life problems and issues.

When people view fantasy as reality, and the fantasy they view constantly pushes a negative message of discord, division and actions that are not conducive to a stable society, is it any wonder Western society has fallen so far? It is worth noting that over seventeen million people tuned in to watch *Coronation Street* to see how the aforementioned story played out – the people being affected by this nonsense are not simply an isolated minority.

Not all people watch soaps though and many people can still see that a soap opera is a work of fiction. But it isn't just fictional works of television and film that seek to warp the mind of Western man – news and current affairs programmes are also used to the same effect. The very programmes that are meant to report the news insert political and social messages into their commentary which are invariably unconducive to a healthy Western mind and the continued existence of Western man.

The news is always told from a narrow perspective and current affairs are always presented within a narrow political spectrum that always leans to the left. Political commentators are nearly always on board with the message that the enemies of the West wish to push, and on the rare occasion when a dissenting voice is allowed to challenge the prevailing dogma, that voice is quickly shouted down and ridiculed. Current affairs shows and debates even go as far as having specially selected audiences that cheer and boo on demand in order to give the appearance that the public support the charade that is taking place.

These controlled debates and narrow discussions on current affairs and the state of the nation are to give the illusion of choice. Again Western man believes he is free; Western man believes there is choice and believes that there is genuine discourse between those who hold different opinions. However this discourse is no different than watching a choreographed fight where the outcome is predetermined. In current affairs debates all roads end up leading to the same destination – whilst at the same time giving the illusion of freedom and choice.

The Western mind has been broken by a sustained attack by the media. Not only has the message presented by the media been negative and destructive, but that message has consistently become more and more negative and destructive over time.

The enemies of the West have been ever more audacious in pushing the envelope and consistently pushed the boundaries of taste, plumbing new lows with each passing year. Yet despite the media's output becoming ever more degenerate, the core message has remained the same – it has always been one designed to undermine and break the Western superego.

The truly shocking revelation surrounding the media's control of Western man's mind is witnessed in the fact that huge numbers of Western people can no longer differentiate fantasy from reality. The public sit glued to their televisions believing that what actors portray on the screen is actually real. This is the extent to which Western man has been brainwashed and his mind warped. Western man will never sit in chains and shackles made of iron, because they are not necessary. Western man already sits in a cage that has been constructed in his own mind – Western man is a prisoner of the media.

If Western man is to ever free himself and rise again, his first step must be to break the mental chains placed upon him. Western man must free his mind and clear the misty fog that clouds his judgement. To defeat the enemies of the West, Western man must first be able to see through the lies he has been told and understand the pitfalls placed in front of him. The first thing Western man must do is break free from the media's iron grip.

15
THE LOSS OF THE WESTERN BODY

The health of any group, society or nation depends on both the physical and mental health of the people who make up that group, society or nation. The great civilisations that grew and prospered did so because of the quality of the people that built them. Strong and physically healthy people build great civilisations – weak, sick and feeble people build nothing.

Once a great civilisation has risen, it takes equally strong people to defend that civilisation. As a civilisation rises and the accomplishments of that civilisation become ever greater, the enemies of that civilisation become ever more eager to tear it down. It follows that if the people that build great civilisations become weak, sick and feeble then it is only a matter of time before those civilisations fall prey to their enemies.

The strength and steel of the Western body was forged in the early days of Western man. When the earliest of Western man's ancestors lived in the harsh frozen lands of Northern Europe the stage was set for only the strongest and most industrious to survive. Those who couldn't survive the biting cold, dig through the frozen ground or hunt in the harsh conditions were doomed and their bloodlines were wiped out as they didn't survive or were unable to ensure the survival of their offspring.

This brutal natural selection process led to several traits – the inventiveness of the Western mind, the drive to form the nuclear family and of course the development of great physical strength and fitness that allowed Western man to cope with the environment in which he lived. As Western man learned to be inventive and industrious and as Western man learned to form lifelong bonds with his partners and to protect his offspring, he also learned to be physically strong.

As time moved on the strong and healthy Western body that had been forged in the harsh environmental conditions of Northern Europe saw Western man become a mighty warrior that dominated the battlefield. Western man not only built great civilisations and fought great wars with his neighbours, but he also conquered and colonised the rest of the world. Once these great gains were made, Western man then needed to defend his expanded territory – often against overwhelming odds. None of these achievements would have been possible if the Western body had been weak, sick or feeble.

Western man's achievements were not confined simply to the battlefield. Western man was also a great explorer – not content with his immediate horizon he sought to expand those horizons until every corner of the globe had been discovered. From Vasco da Gama who discovered the sea route to India, to Christopher Columbus who discovered the Americas, to Robert Falcon Scott who led expeditions to Antarctica and to Edmund Hillary who was the first man to climb Mount Everest, Western man discovered the world and conquered its harshest environments.

These incredible achievements were not the feats of weak men, but were achieved by those who had great physical and mental fortitude. What's more, these great feats were achieved without the advanced technology of the modern era. Journey by sea was treacherous and ships were manned by crews who were pushed to their physical limits, limits that would be tested even further when they reached their destinations and mounted brave and daring expeditions through uncharted territories.

The enemies of any nation know that to weaken the bodies of the people who make up that nation would undermine the nation itself. By making a people weak, by robbing them of their ability to defend themselves and by poisoning or breaking their bodies, the community in which those people live is put at risk and becomes increasingly attractive prey to potential predators. But how can the enemies of the West effectively go about weakening the physical form of Western man?

As discussed earlier, the first logical place to strike is the mind, as once the mind is reduced in its capacity to reason and the hardened mental fortitude of a people is turned to jelly, those people can be convinced of anything. The attack on the Western body has intensified as the Western mind has been overcome.

A weakened mental state allows for a subject to be manipulated far more easily. Once the mind has been conquered, unhealthy ideas and theories which would once have been disregarded by an able mind can easily be implanted and seen as healthy. Whereas the healthy mind will reject notions that would lead to the harm of the individual and the destruction of the individual's body, the unhealthy mind can easily be persuaded that these destructive notions are in fact sound.

The old phrase 'healthy mind, healthy body' rings true. When the mind is healthy, so will be the body as the outward reflection of inner mental health and strength is a strong and healthy body. The enemies of the West know this, they also know that by defeating both the mind and the body of Western man, Western man will completely be at the mercy of his enemies and simply be a shadow of his former self.

To convince a sane man to ingest poison and to convince him to commit insane and self-destructive acts would be difficult if nigh-on impossible. However to convince an insane man to ingest poison and harm himself through self-destructive acts would be like pushing at an open door. The enemies of the West know this and that is why they set about destroying Western man's mind first and foremost, as with the mind broken it would then be so much easier to destroy Western man's once healthy body.

Just as Western man has been enslaved by subtle and devious means and held in servitude by invisible chains and cages that exist only in his mind, Western man's body is not poisoned by force either. No one is dragged off to medical facilities and tied to beds to have their poison administered by force; no one has their nose held and the poison poured down their throat against their will. In fact quite the opposite is true, Western man takes his own poison without the need for force as he wilfully destroys his own body in acts that amount to no more than self-harm.

The once proud, strong and healthy Western warrior and explorer is now an obese and unhealthy slob confined to his couch as those who control the mass media pump ever more garbage into his head as he shovels ever more garbage into his mouth. As a result of this, the Western population's level of physical fitness has declined dramatically over the last few decades, and the size of Western man's waist has increased considerably.

The changing shape and the attitude to the changing shape of Western man can most easily be illustrated by looking at an interesting relic of our past – the carnival freak show. At the beginning of the 20th century these freak shows toured Western nations displaying the odd and the perverse. It was not uncommon for these freak shows to feature a 'fat man', who patrons of the carnival found unbelievable.

The 'fat man' was considered freakish and large beyond belief and average-sized folks actually paid for the privilege of looking at him. Yet by today's standard the 'fat man' would seem normal and one would not have to pay to see him. In fact one would only need to take a trip to any supermarket where dozens of hugely obese men and women could be observed filling their trollies with mountains of sugary and fatty snacks that have little nutritional value and act as a slow-working poison on the individual's once healthy body.

The enemies of the West have pushed the envelope with health just as they pushed the envelope with the poison they poured into the Western mind. Just as it became acceptable to push ever more degenerate nonsense in both music and film, it has become more and more acceptable to become increasingly unhealthy. This acceptance for obesity and unhealthy living has even culminated in what is termed the 'body acceptance' movement.

The Western obesity epidemic is not just reducing the capacity of Western man as a fighter, a pioneer and an explorer – but it also brings with it a myriad of health problems. Obesity literally destroys the human body and places massive strain on the structures and organs within leading to heart disease, respiratory problems, diabetes and a weakened immune system. In extreme cases obesity can even lead to problems of a greater magnitude which actually reduce the individual to being bedridden resulting in that individual being as helpless as a newborn child and requiring round-the-clock care.

This kind of gluttony represents another triumph of the id over the superego. Eating is a natural drive and as such is governed by the id; it is a desire that we wish to satisfy and when that desire is satisfied we feel good. However a developed superego would control the desire to eat and curb overindulgence. Once the superego is weakened and the id can take control, we seek constant satisfaction and as a result the individual simply eats as a form of pleasure without a thought for the consequences.

The id is of course only concerned with short-term immediate satisfaction – and as such needs to be constrained. The id is selfish and greedy and not concerned with longer term goals and prospects. Few actions illustrate this as well as gluttony – the short-term desire to fulfil the urge to eat and to gain endless pleasure from overeating are in complete contradiction to the long-term welfare, health and survival of the individual.

A developed superego is our morality and thus keeps the id in check and reminds us not to be greedy and gluttonous. The developed superego also contains our vision of our ideal self to which we work toward becoming – and what could be less of an ideal self than a bloated, greedy, unfit individual who is plagued by health problems? Yet increasingly, Western man is that bloated individual, and that represents a triumph for both the id and the enemies of the West.

But greed often goes hand in hand with laziness, and where food is concerned nothing could be more evident. Not only are people eating far more – what they are eating is far worse for them. The drive for quick and easy satisfaction from food has led to the increasing availability of unhealthy 'fast food' laden with chemical preservatives, artificial flavours, huge amounts of sugar and salt and very little genuine nutritional value.

These artificial foods are very much like drugs – they give an instant sugary and chemical high which sets the pleasure receptors in the brain alight. But that buzz soon wears off, and unlike a healthy meal that can satisfy an individual for the best part of a day, unhealthy snacks only provide short-term satisfaction and soon leave the individual craving more of the same. Just like a drug user, the food addict craves more and ever larger portions of unhealthy food in a desperate effort to satisfy their cravings.

Of course, these unhealthy options are also constantly promoted by the enemies of the West through the television and the media. The Western mind is bombarded with adverts – many of which are aimed at young children in order to corrupt their young minds and get them hooked early on poisonous junk food and unhealthy snacks.

It is not enough that Western folk are being poisoned and turned from healthy people into an overweight and unhealthy collection of food addicts – but now the same people who gave us bad role models, media poison and feminism now tell us that fat is 'beautiful' and health can come at any size. As Western beauty and femininity is attacked through degrading sexual practices in pornography, it is also attacked through the promotion of unhealthy living and obesity.

The Western female was deified for her beauty and her femininity, inspiring generations of Western society and being the subject of Western poetry, song, literature and art. Whilst the Western female had natural curves, she was not covered in rolls of unsightly fat. To see a bloated and swollen female is to see a perversion of beauty, a twisted vision of what women should aim to be and what men should aspire to be with.

Yet now feminists and those behind the negative role models foisted upon our youth give us the 'plus sized' model, 'fat activist' and the aforementioned body acceptance movement. The plus sized model is in itself an oxymoron – a model is by its very definition 'a thing used as an example to follow or imitate'. How on earth is an overweight, greedy, self-indulgent and unhealthy individual an 'example to follow or imitate'? The answer is simple – they are not, but neither are the other role models being pushed upon impressionable young minds.

The feminist will be quick to tell you that it is not obesity that is the problem, but in fact anorexia and bulimia are what plague the modern female, and the cause of these plagues is an unscrupulous and male-dominated fashion industry. This can be easily debunked as less than one per cent of the population suffer from those forms of eating disorder, compared to 67 per cent of men and 57 per cent of women being either overweight or obese. Anorexia and bulimia are terrible mental issues, but they are not a plague on society of the same scale as obesity.

Obesity and an unhealthy body do not just affect Western man on an individual level but affect Western society as a group. The obesity epidemic most obviously robs Western man of his ability to defend his community against prospective threats as his once warrior-like body is no longer fit and able to go to war. However there is also a deeper implication to the obesity epidemic that affects community cohesion.

Humans are social creatures and they form bonds with one another – those bonds and repeated social interactions lead to communities forming. However when people are obese they are less likely to go out, less likely to interact and more likely to spend time alone doing sedentary and solitary activities which serve to further isolate the individual from their community. But is this not what the enemies of the West wish for? The once great Western man sits isolated in his own home, separated from his community as he lounges on his sofa eating what amounts to poison as he stares intently at a flickering screen which imparts destructive messages that were created to warp the Western mind.

When children grow up in broken homes more often than not they lack discipline, authority and a strong male role model, these factors have a profound effect on the development of the child's superego. Children are now increasingly likely to grow up in homes where obesity is seen as normal – this too has a profound effect on a child's mental development. Children base their vision of an ideal self on their parents – so the message imparted to children that grow up with fat parents is that obesity is normal; obesity then becomes part of that child's ideal self. What could be more damaging to the future physical and mental health of a child than to normalise the self-destructive act of overeating?

The obesity epidemic not only robs Western man of his ability to fight and undermines community cohesion, but it also robs Western man of his ability to reproduce. Obesity is known to be linked with a reduced fertility rate – and a low birth rate is already a critical problem faced by Western man. By literally poisoning their bodies with unhealthy food, Western males and Western females have reduced their capacity to bear children. Not only is the Western mind being twisted to see childrearing as undesirable, but Western man is increasingly physically unable to procreate.

However greed, obesity and fast food is not the only threat to Western man's body. A rapid increase in size may be the biggest and most obvious change Western man's body has undergone, but the negative role models pushed upon younger generations are quick to promote other vices that can destroy the body and tear apart a community far quicker than junk food and excess weight.

Both alcohol abuse and drug abuse have dramatically increased in Western society and have taken hold of younger generations as negative role models have glorified substance abuse, binge drinking and a hedonistic 'party' lifestyle. As discussed before, role models that are promoted in both film and music have always pushed the themes of rebellion and living for the moment without a thought for the consequences.

Often these role models are fictional characters like Jim Stark in *Rebel Without a Cause* or Telly and Casper in the film *Kids*. Characters that appear in film and on television promote negative pursuits within a fictional setting – as discussed earlier fantasy and reality are becoming increasingly blurred in the mind of Western man. But despite this, these fictional role models do not directly interact with the public. However role models like film stars and pop stars are different to fictional characters as they do exist in reality and can interact directly with their fans.

Role models like Lady Gaga, Katy Perry and Rhianna (or their male counterparts) can have a greater, longer lasting and more influential relationship with their fans than fictional characters. As they are real people they exist outside of a single film, series of books or television programme and can thus have a more direct relationship with those who look up to them. These real life role models have every facet of their lives played out in the media – letting every impressionable young mind know of their every depraved and degenerate act.

Let's look at one particular singer – Amy Winehouse. Amy Winehouse was a drug user and alcoholic. She ruined her career as a singer and ultimately died because of the choices she made. She died a pitiful death and in her last months her body was racked with the signs of drug and alcohol abuse. A healthy society would not hold Amy Winehouse up as a role model and certainly wouldn't expose youngsters to the self-destructive lifestyle she chose to embrace.

As the enemies of the West seek to push negative role models upon Western youth, Amy Winehouse is now held up as a national hero. She is a darling of the nation and in North London a statue was erected to commemorate her life. Statues should be reserved for those who have given something of great worth to society and acted in a selfless and exemplary fashion. Amy Winehouse did none of those things; she followed her id and acted in a selfish manner, only seeking her own immediate pleasure without sparing a thought for the consequences of her actions.

What's more, Amy Winehouse wasn't a 'down and out' who was born into a difficult life and used drugs as a means of escape. She was born into a wealthy family and had every opportunity in life; what's more her career in music made her a millionaire. Amy

Winehouse had no excuses and none should be made on her behalf. What message does it send to young people when they see Amy Winehouse has been honoured with a statue? Amy Winehouse had it all, she wanted for nothing and she also had a gift to share – but instead of grasping her opportunities she squandered them all for the short-term gain associated with alcohol, drugs and partying.

As future generations are increasingly ravaged by alcohol and substance abuse, questions are often asked as to why young people increasingly choose such a destructive path. Well for those seeking the answer, look no further than the statue of Amy Winehouse in North London. Ask yourself the question, if the youth of today had a choice between looking up to the statue of Horatio Nelson or looking up to the statue of Amy Winehouse, which would serve them better as a source of inspiration?

A healthy body was necessary for Western man to build such mighty civilisations – but a healthy body was also necessary in order to successfully defend those civilisations. A healthy body allowed Western man to fulfil his potential and follow his dreams – a healthy body allowed Western man to explore the world and conquer his adversaries. No other culture or race could have stood against Western man and as a result Western civilisation was never seen as an easy target to those who looked on in envy at what Western man had created.

But just as Western man's inventive and intelligent mind has been polluted and poisoned by those who seek to destroy Western civilisation, so has Western man's body been polluted and poisoned. This has not been achieved through force but through guile; Western man has been subtly coerced into poisoning himself. Without moral values and a strong superego, Western man has given in to his base desire to seek short-term pleasure. Western society is now plagued by obesity and Western youth are increasingly turning to drugs and alcohol.

The once mighty Western warrior sits isolated in his armchair watching images flicker across an electronic screen as he ingests ever more sugary and fatty poison. Is it any wonder other cultures and races now view Western man with contempt? The people who once looked at Western civilisation with envy now look at Western man with derision and a mocking smirk.

Western man must rediscover his roots and reconnect with natural food and natural healthy pursuits and once again take up the struggle of self-improvement in order to better himself. If the time ever comes where you are forced to defend yourself and your loved ones, make sure you can do so to the best of your ability. It is better to die on your feet with your sword in your hand as you defend your loved ones than to sit in your armchair as a helpless and bloated slob as your family and community perish!

16

THE LOSS OF THE
WESTERN SOUL

The existence of the soul is something that has been long debated by religious scholars, philosophers and scientists. Does the soul exist and what does its existence signify? In a very real sense, the soul is a deeper level of consciousness that lies at the very core of our being. It is that special extra 'something' that sets us apart from other creatures in the animal kingdom. The soul is the spiritual or immaterial part of a human being.

The soul is often seen as immortal, something that transcends life and death and lives on for eternity. The idea of the soul has been with us from the beginning of recorded time and probably existed long before that. Whilst in many ways the soul can be seen as intangible, it is often seen as the 'breath of life' that animates the body – in effect the very essence of the human being.

The soul is separate and distinct from the body and the mind. You can feed and satisfy your body through food and physical activity. You can satisfy your mind through knowledge and discovery. But to satisfy the soul, that is a deeper and altogether more complex affair. To satisfy the soul is in many ways more important than either physical or mental satisfaction, as a satisfied soul leads to one being at peace with both himself and the world around him.

Once the soul is at ease and satisfied other stresses and pains seem less significant. The importance of achieving spiritual satisfaction is in many ways more important than simply satisfying the mind and body. An individual that endlessly seeks spiritual satisfaction but never finds it ends up feeling spiritually restless which can lead to a tortured existence. An individual who finds the search for inner peace to be elusive would live a truly cursed existence.

If an individual has a restless soul and constantly searches for inner peace, that quest will hamper the individual's ability to achieve other goals. For a man cannot be at ease with his surroundings, his peers and most crucially not even be at ease with himself when he harbours a restless soul. Logically, when a man is not at ease with himself, he can never be truly free or happy. What's more, when an individual's soul is not at ease all the other problems that individual faces seem magnified.

The soul is a higher form of consciousness and thus not directly observable which in turn makes it hard to study in a scientific way. The soul is not something we can see, measure or directly quantify or catalogue – in these ways the soul is very much like the superego. As we know what causes the superego to develop, we can assess the influences that feed the soul and provide spiritual nourishment.

Broadly speaking there are three different spiritual bonds that serve to feed the soul and satisfy spiritual needs. The more these bonds are strengthened and the more the soul is satisfied, the more at ease one becomes with both himself and the world around him. A happy and spiritually fulfilled individual has the foundations for success in life, as positive mental and physical growth are much more likely to occur in individuals that are at peace with themselves.

The first and most fundamental spiritual bond that feeds the soul is the bond that an individual shares with their immediate family, loved ones and with members of the community in which they live. This bond comes from human interaction with loved ones, the people that you hold the most dear and those you identify most strongly with. This most fundamental spiritual need springs forth from the nuclear family and its roots lie in the development of the family bonds that Western man began to form and develop during the earliest days of Western society.

As males and females form complementary pairs that eventually become more than the sum of their constituent parts, a major part of spiritual fulfilment comes from finding a life partner. As stated before, the bonds we form with our life partners are based on more than simple attraction, sexual chemistry and the desire to procreate. Humans develop a powerful emotion which acts as a bond for life between two loving partners – that emotion is love.

Love is one of the basic spiritual bonds that feed the soul. We also feel love for our parents and, in time when we go on to become parents ourselves, we feel love for our children. This powerful emotion is something that makes our soul feel at ease and makes us feel as though we belong when we are around our loved ones. When around those we love and around those who love us, we feel at home. The old phrase 'home is where the heart is' would be more accurately stated as 'home is where the soul is most at ease'.

People yearn to be around their families and loved ones and are drawn back to them when they are separated. This is why death takes such a toll on any close family, as losing a loved one for good feels as though you are not just losing another person, but that you are losing part of yourself too – something that takes a toll on one's soul. These natural bonds are extended to those within a close and cohesive community – friends, relatives and those within the community who are looked up to and respected.

As we mature, we search for a partner, and the natural urge is to have children and pass on our genetics to the next generation. Immense spiritual fulfilment comes from raising children. To see the product of your love for another human expressed in the form of a child – your son or daughter – is overwhelming. To hold in your arms a tiny and helpless child, a child that is entirely dependent on your love and care and a child that carries your blood, is an experience that changes a person and fulfils them in a way that cannot be matched by other achievements.

A strong family and strong parents help a child to develop, teaching that child the ways of life. There can be few things more spiritually fulfilling than seeing your own child grow and develop under your tutelage – eventually becoming a strong upstanding adult who carries on the family lineage. These experiences and the bonds that a parent shares with a child are truly spiritual experiences and satisfy and feed the soul.

To lack these family and community bonds, to be a loner or an outsider and to never feel love or to never pass on your blood must be a terrible burden for the soul and lead to feelings of isolation and deep depression – something that would cause the soul to cry out in pain.

The second broad group of spiritual bonds that feed the soul come from our connection to the environment and the natural world around us. We evolved in the natural world and around nature, and thus we are a product of nature and our development is intrinsically tied to the natural world. If the bond to our family and community is important, so is the bond to the world around us that provides for us. If you look at earth as a mother – mother earth – she is the mother of Western man and she provides for us in every way.

We are a product of our environment; we have discussed this at length and we have discussed how the unique environment of Northern Europe shaped Western man into what he became and gifted him with the traits that allowed him to build such advanced civilisations. Western man's struggle with the environment in which he lived was difficult, but over time Western man emerged from that struggle with a deep understanding of both himself and the world in which he lived.

Nature provided for Western man – the wood for his fires to keep him warm, the plants for his food, the animals that were both his companions and his livestock and the water which quenched his thirst. Everything Western man had and everything Western man built came from nature in one way or another. Wood, stone and metal all came from the earth and Western man used these natural resources to raise up Western society and to build the great civilisations that stand to this day.

The bonds Western man shared with his environment and the natural world have slowly been weakened as Western man has grown more technologically advanced. As we have divorced ourselves from the natural world and cocooned ourselves in manmade and unnatural environments, we have seen a huge rise in depression – depression of course comes from a soul that is not spiritually fulfilled. We do not gain the same level of natural satisfaction and spiritual fulfilment trapped indoors starring at a screen as we do from being outside in the natural world.

These bonds with nature were always emphasised by the ancestors of Western man and until very recently there was always a huge drive to get young people out into the natural world. Scouting groups would regularly take children camping, hunting and fishing as a way of connecting them with their natural environment and aiding their spiritual development.

It is also testament to the natural bonds Western man has with the environment that many traditional Western pastimes – the pursuits that took place in one's free time in order to recharge the spiritual batteries and give folk a sense of belonging – took place outside. Hunting, fishing, hiking, exploring and sleeping out under the stars all connected Western man not only with nature, but also with the ways of his ancestors and their more natural ways of living.

There are few things more spiritually uplifting than walking through the forest as the sun shines down through the trees casting light on the flowers that gather across the forest floor as the birds sing in the trees and the fresh scent of a summer's morning drifts through the air. The very thought of such a thing is uplifting and calming to the soul.

The final of the three broad groups of spiritual bonds that feed the soul is religion and one's deeper spiritual beliefs in a god or an afterlife. Religion can be both contentious and highly divisive, but religion is also something that played a huge part in the development of the Western world as Western man sought to make sense of things such as the existence of the soul and the circle of life and death.

Even primitive man held religious beliefs – whether that was the worship of the sun, the moon and the seasons, or the worship of gods associated with different facets of the natural world such as the land, sea and air. There were the religions of ancient Greece, Egypt, Rome and Scandinavia as well as the pagan beliefs of the tribes native to the British Isles. These beliefs changed and evolved over time and some disappeared and were replaced by Christianity as it spread across the West.

The purpose of this is not to examine different religions in detail or to say which religion is right, or in fact which religion is wrong – but simply to state that religion has always played a central part in feeding the soul and providing spiritual nourishment for

Western man. Religion has sought to explain the soul and give Western man faith in the idea of the immortality of the soul – a belief shared by ancient philosophers such as Socrates and Plato.

Religion has bound communities together and sought to give them moral guidance as well as spiritual guidance. It has given people inner strength and helped them deal with the death of loved ones and other personal losses. Crucially, religion has sought to remove the fear of death and give people faith that there is more to life than simply survival – that there is a higher spiritual meaning to life and that we do not merely exist in the here and now, and will not merely be washed away like grains of sand on a beach.

The importance of spiritual pursuits and beliefs are clear, as is the importance of the spiritual bonds that exist in order to feed the Western soul. Spiritual bonds tie Western man to his immediate family, those within his community and to the natural world around him. Just as the enemies of the West have attacked the body and mind of Western man, they also wish to attack Western spirituality and mount an assault on the Western soul. The enemies of the West have enslaved the Western mind and they have poisoned the body of Western man, but they have also weakened the spiritual bonds that feed the Western soul.

The family unit and the community which it is part of, Western man's connection with the natural environment and Western religious institutions and spiritual beliefs have all been under relentless attack and have been undermined and weakened. But the enemies of the West always have something else up their sleeves – whenever they create a vacuum by removing a positive, they always seek to fill that vacuum with something unnatural and unhealthy that only serves to further enslave Western man.

As the influences in our lives that give us spiritual fulfilment have been slowly dismantled and removed, we have been presented with a spiritually worthless alternative that has been pushed relentlessly by the enemies of the West – that bankrupt alternative is materialism. The new 'spiritual' pursuit of the West is to spend money and to acquire material objects – and the more we spend and the more we acquire the better we are meant to feel. Materialism is the belief that the acquisition of physical objects is the route to lasting happiness; but nothing could be further from the truth.

Material objects can make us happy and they can bring us enjoyment in the short term – but they can never bring the deep lasting happiness that is gained from true spiritual fulfilment. Material objects are a means to an end; they serve a purpose and a function – of course one can take pride in those objects and one can take pleasure in some of them, but that pride and pleasure will never replace genuine spiritual fulfilment.

For example, one can purchase a dinner table, chairs and the best dining set that money can buy. But ultimately those goods are limited – the plates may be aesthetically perfect and the knives and forks wonderfully crafted, but if the food eaten with them is subpar the quality of the plates and cutlery makes little difference. Equally, a magnificent table and well-crafted chairs may be both comfortable and pleasing to the eye, but without friends to sit in the chairs and family to gather around the table, their worth is significantly diminished.

A man can purchase an expensive luxury car and can surely derive pleasure from driving it, but if the journey he makes is lonely and he is headed to a place where he is neither loved nor wanted then surely he would be happier to walk barefoot in the rain to a warm home full of people he loved and who eagerly anticipated his arrival. These examples are simple, but they illustrate an important point – that it is not material goods alone that make us happy, but who we share them with that is important. This leads us back to the real path to spiritual fulfilment – our connection to the people we love and our bond to our ancestral homeland, yet sadly those connections have been weakened and in some cases have been completely severed.

Instead of following spiritual pursuits, people now live for the acquisition of material items and every week millions flock to department stores, supermarkets and shopping centres in order to spend money on items they believe will enhance their lives and bring them happiness. These temples of consumerism are neither homely, natural nor are they in any way spiritual – yet they have become the new places of worship for Western man. As cashiers ring up endless transactions, the consumer clamours to purchase items in a vain attempt to fill the void they feel at the centre of their soul, a void created by their neglect of genuine spiritual pursuits.

In the short term these purchased items do bring excitement and happiness and a small buzz – but soon that buzz wears off. In the modern world everything is readily available and as a result people are used to excess and accustomed to getting exactly what they desire. This lack of scarcity ensures the individual does not cherish the items they purchase as they might cherish a family heirloom passed down from generation to generation. Everything is disposable and this is reflected in the way we treat our possessions. A key part of the problem we face is that we rarely need what we buy. We buy items because we want them, not because we need them; our desires are not driven by necessity but by materialistic greed.

As the items we purchase no longer mean anything to us and the products we crave do not bring lasting happiness, we increasingly discard and disrespect our possessions. Soon people are not buying items because they need them or even because they want them – they are buying for the sake of buying. We have become habituated to walking around shopping centres at the weekend spending money on whatever grabs our attention as we crave the instant gratification we gain from the act of purchasing on impulse.

But that is the problem – we have started to derive pleasure from the act of buying itself – and the more we spend and the higher the bill, the more we feel we are elevated above others around us. People now compete with one another based on what they have purchased and how much money they have spent. Western man has become a slave to consumerism – buying for the sake of buying in order gain attention and one-upmanship over one's peers.

This grotesque materialism is endorsed by bad role models and reinforced by the vacuous celebrity culture that influences the mind of Western man. Bizarre social rules emerge; females are told they should never wear the same dress twice, men are told that the price of their bar tab is a status symbol and far more important than the taste of the liquor being drunk, and we are all told that the number of bags we carry home is directly proportional to our level of happiness. This warped morality colours our vision and affects the way we value everything in our lives: materialism has become Western man's new god!

So as Western man rushes to worship at the temple of materialism, he spends, spends and spends some more until he has nothing left. Then he spends some more – because why should he save for something he can have tomorrow when he can borrow the shortfall and have what he desires today? This is exactly what the enemies of the West have planned, and in Western man's rush to own everything and keep up with his neighbours, he applies for credit cards, payday loans and borrows from wherever he can. Western man is then reduced to no more than a financial slave, forever in the debt of shady money lenders and crooks.

As Western man's pursuit of materialism intensifies, his debts rise. Western man finds himself with less and less disposable income and this financial pressure begins to affect his personal relationships, often forcing Western man to the suicidal conclusion that he can't afford to breed. After all what could be a bigger financial commitment than a child? Not only has Western man replaced true spirituality with the pursuit of materialism, but Western man has allowed materialism to become a barrier to the most natural callings in life – building a family and having children.

Materialism controls us and it moulds our thinking, turning us into greedy and shallow individuals obsessed with material objects, this obsession consumes us and keeps us from engaging in genuinely fulfilling pursuits. Western man pours increasingly large sums of money into the pursuit of materialism, often forcing himself into debt in a vain and pointless attempt to be the envy of his neighbours.

But materialism is an empty and soulless pursuit – no matter how much money you pour into that pot it will never be full. Eventually when there is no money left and debts begin mounting, the goods acquired during the mad spending sprees are of little or no consolation and the pressure of the debt and the resulting depression takes its toll. In our race to fill the spiritual void left by the loss of family bonds, our bond with the natural world, and our religious and spiritual beliefs, we have ended up worshiping a false idol.

Again we see the triumph of the id – immediate pleasure derived from spending money that we don't have is put before our own long-term financial stability. The superego imparts control, conscience and allows us to reason on a moral level. Once the superego is damaged and the id reigns, we give in to impulsive drives and think only of short-term pleasure.

The enemies of the West must be rubbing their hands with glee. The once great Western man, mentally enslaved, physically enfeebled and spiritually bereft – but also financially shackled and in debt to the very people who wish to see the West fall.

Western man needs to rediscover what makes him whole – the things that spiritually feed him and complete his soul allowing him to be at ease with himself and his surroundings. Western man needs to throw off the shackles of materialism and pursue genuine spirituality – through the bonds with his family, his environment and through his religious beliefs.

The void we feel at the centre of our very being cannot be filled with material goods; as such our devotion to materialism must be broken. Materialism is not a means to an end; it is a means to enslave Western man through usury and debt.

17

THE LOSS OF THE WESTERN HEART

The Western heart is not just Western man's love for his family and his folk, but it encompasses something much more important. The Western heart stems from Western man's love for his people and it is what drives Western man to protect those people at all costs. The Western heart can be summed up quite simply as Western man's courage and bravery, which are the traits that allow Western man to go that step further when necessary to defend his blood and soil. The Western heart has been a major contributing factor in the development of Western civilisation.

History books are full of the tales of Western heart, bravery and courage. This bravery and courage allowed Western man to stand strong even in the face of overwhelming odds; it allowed Western man to undertake great challenges even when the risk of failure or death was high, and it ensured that Western man protected his loved ones and community at any cost. The Western heart was the heart of a warrior, an explorer and a pioneer. The Western heart drove Western civilisation forward and protected that civilisation from those who wished to tear it down.

There are many examples of Western heart throughout the illustrious history of Western civilisation and even from the earliest recorded history these acts of courage can be seen – the Battle of Thermopylae is a perfect example. Three hundred brave Spartan warriors and a small group of allies were vastly outnumbered by the Persian army, yet despite the odds being heavily stacked against them, the courage and the bravery of the Spartans went down in history as they broke the spirit of the Persian invaders. Despite the Spartans ultimately perishing, their actions bought the Greek nations enough time to rally and eventually defeat the Persian Empire.

The Battle of Vienna is another great example of Western bravery and courage. Again Western man found himself outnumbered five to one against the vast forces of the Ottoman Empire. This battle was a decisive one and marked the turning point in the Ottoman-Habsburg wars, a three hundred-year struggle between the Holy Roman and Ottoman empires. This great victory led to the collapse of the Turkish occupation of Eastern Europe and allowed Western man to regain control over his homeland.

Another fine example of Western heart was seen at the Battle of Rorke's Drift. Just over one hundred and fifty British and colonial troops successfully defended the garrison at the mission station at Rorke's Drift against an intense assault by three to four thousand Zulu warriors. Again, Western man was vastly outnumbered yet stood firm in the face of overwhelming odds and what would have seemed like a fate of certain death.

These brave actions – and many more like them – shaped the West and held the rest of the world in awe of Western man's bravery and courage. The common factor in these acts of bravery was that the men who stood firm faced almost certain death at the hands of their enemies. The odds were stacked so heavily against them that defeat looked almost certain, yet even in the face of defeat and death Western man stood strong and looked his enemy in the eye and fought on regardless.

These acts of bravery are the embodiment of the Western heart and the motivation for these acts stem from Western man's love for those he protects and his duty to his community. Such was Western man's commitment to his community and fellow man, that to turn and flee and to leave the field of combat would have been unthinkable – Western man would rather stand and fight to the death than let down his comrades and his community. The Western heart is again the product of a developed superego. In this case the superego is so strong it not only overrides the id, but actually overrides the ego too, putting the individual in mortal danger. This illustrates the strength of the superego and the strength of the commitment Western man once had to his community.

The Western heart is something that has always stood in the way of the enemies of the West. The Western heart has galvanised Western man and ensured that he would always stand and fight for what was right – for the defence of his loved ones, his community and his nation. The enemies of the West know that to break the Western heart, to remove that bravery and courage that has seen the West weather so many invasions and threats, would be to break the inner steel of Western man and rob him of the ability to protect his people.

The enemies of the West have concocted the most devious of schemes in order to break the Western heart. Just like many of their other plots, this scheme begins with their careful use of the media and the promotion of bad role models which are designed to warp the Western mind. Once the Western mind is broken the enemies of the West can manipulate all facets of Western man. This is exactly how the enemies of the West have sought to undermine the Western heart and this attack can be summed up in two words – white guilt.

To make a race or culture hate themselves would be the most powerful way to ensure the destruction of that race or culture as it would rob them of their ability to defend themselves and even cause that race or culture to wish for their own destruction. This feeling of self-hatred has been instilled in Western man by a prolonged and sustained campaign of lies and half-truths intended to make Western man feel guilty for everything he has accomplished, everything he is and ultimately for even merely existing.

Those who control the media and those who have undermined and hijacked the education system have slowly introduced this guilt and self-loathing into almost every level of Western consciousness. This has been done through several highly effective attacks which have originated from twisted portrayals of slavery, the West's colonial past and of course the holy grail of guilt and self-loathing – the holocaust.

By rewriting history or by presenting historical snapshots in a manner where they are no longer viewed within the correct context or from the correct perspective, the enemies of the West have managed to ensure that generations of Western youth actively despise their own ancestors. This is of course an attack on the superego, as the superego is a way of preserving morals, values and traditions and ensuring they are passed down from generation to generation. By making the young distrust or despise their own ancestors ensures the death of tradition and heritage, as who would want to follow in the footsteps of those they hated?

Slavery is the first and most obvious attack on the Western heart and something that every Western child is made to feel guilty for. Before we go into any historical detail, on a purely logical level, why should any Western man feel guilty for slavery? There is no Western man alive who owns an African slave – equally there is no African alive who is owned or ever has been owned by a Western man. So why on earth should Western man feel guilt for something he personally played no part in – or should the son pay for the sins of his father?

Strangely enough, those who insist that Western man should pay for the sins of his forefathers, both through financial reparations and the burden of eternal guilt, are the same people who tell Western man that being proud of the positive achievements of his ancestors is both pointless and illogical! So whilst Western man cannot show any pride for the achievements of his ancestors, he can certainly feel guilt and shame for their alleged crimes.

Alleged crimes is exactly the point though, as the acts Western man is accused of perpetrating are often utterly distorted or taken so far out of context that their portrayal borders on fiction. Slavery is a clear case in point. The established narrative on slavery is that the wicked Western man went to the peaceful continent of Africa and rounded up every happy and peace-loving African he could find and forced them into a life of brutal slavery.

It is indeed true that a tiny minority of Western society kept African slaves – however to take this out of its historical context is to begin a dangerous lie that only leads to white guilt and Western self-hatred. In fact in the United States at the peak of the slave trade just 1.6 per cent of the population owned slaves. Slavery has existed from the beginning of recorded history and every racial or ethnic group has at one time or another either owned slaves or been enslaved themselves. Slavery existed in biblical times, in ancient Mesopotamia, in ancient Egypt, in Rome and throughout the Middle Ages.

Both slaves and slave traders have come in every colour, and slaves were often the product of war – a conquered tribe would often be enslaved by those who conquered them, in effect making slaves a spoil of war. Does this make slavery right? Of course it doesn't. But it does place slavery in the correct and historically accurate context as a social phenomenon that existed on a global scale and not as the enemies of the West wish to portray it. Europeans, Africans, Asians, Arabs and East Asians have all at one time or another owned slaves, yet it is the European who is beaten with the stick of guilt for his participation in the slave trade.

What is even more contradictory about the established truth on slavery and the slave trade is that it was William Wilberforce, an English politician and philanthropist, who led the movement to have slavery abolished. It was Western man who abolished slavery and it was Western man who poured money, resources and troops into ensuring that the practice of slavery was combated on a global scale.

Despite Western man's noble act of opposing slavery and emancipating the slaves owned by those living in Western nations, slavery still exists today. Modern slavery is a multi-billion dollar industry with experts estimating that up to $35 billion is generated annually through the trade. The United Nations estimates that roughly 27 to 30 million men, women and children are currently caught up in the modern slave trade. These slaves are overwhelmingly located in the developing or third world, not Western nations – but the enemies of the West tell us it is Western man who should feel guilty for slavery.

This same theme is expanded to include guilt for Western man's colonial past. Due to the nature of Western man and the fact he was both a pioneer and explorer, it was natural that during exploration Western man formed colonies around the world. Western man colonised Africa, Asia and the Americas and brought advanced civilisation to those continents. As Western man colonised foreign lands, he farmed their plains, fished their waters and mined their resources.

The history of colonisation has been twisted and taken out of context in a similar way to the narrative on slavery, the effect of which is to create a 'black and white' story of Western man raping foreign lands and stealing the resources and the destiny of the native people who were wrongfully disposed of their birth right. However to paint that picture would be dishonest and misleading, as Western man gave much more than he took when he colonised other countries.

Western man shared his great technology with every nation he colonised and used that technology to better the lives of the native people. Western man built schools, hospitals and infrastructure. Western man gave these countries medical care, clean running water and sanitation. Western man introduced written language, the motor car and farming methods that vastly increased the yield of the natives' crops. All of these technological marvels improved the lives of the native people and helped develop their countries. Western man did take resources from the places he colonised, but he gave back just as much as he ever took – if not more.

Yet when the enemies of the West talk of colonisation, they do not talk of the improvements and inventions that Western man gave to the world as that would make today's Western youth proud of their ancestors; the enemies of the West talk only of what Western man took. The younger generations are taught that their ancestors were no better than bullies and common thieves who stole the wealth of peaceful people who were not able defend themselves against Western colonial might. Again this teaches Western man to feel guilt and shame for the actions of his ancestors and ultimately to despise his own lineage.

When it comes to the notion of white guilt, nothing is pushed more strongly nor made more prominent in the minds of Western people than the holocaust. The holocaust is the alleged extermination of six million Jews at the hands of the German people during World War 2. The level of hysteria that surrounds the holocaust is so great that it is actually illegal in many countries to question any aspect of the holocaust's authenticity.

The holocaust is taught in schools and presented in the media as the greatest single act of evil that has ever taken place – and of course, that it was Western man and his drive for nationalism that caused such an evil act to occur. The holocaust has been elevated to a level of importance so great that it has its own worldwide day of remembrance, and a multi-million dollar industry exists to push the established narrative. The holocaust industry churns out movies, books and television shows on a regular basis to ensure that the holocaust is constantly kept in the collective mind of Western man.

The holocaust is particularly important as not only is the holocaust presented as the most evil act to have ever taken place – but the motivation for this act was not simply greed, but Western man's drive for nationalism. So in essence the motto of this story is that Western man's own love for his people and culture and his will for self-determination led directly to the greatest crime to ever have taken place in the history of humanity. The message imparted to future generations is clear – not only should Western man feel guilty for the crimes of his ancestors, but Western man's brutality and cruelty is at its worst when he pursues a path of nationalism.

The important question one must ask is clear: in a world where every single detail of history can be questioned, debated and investigated, why is it that one single historical issue should be off limits for any kind of debate or investigation, and why are those who seek to debate or investigate that issue threatened with the full force of the law and the loss of their liberties?

It is often said that the truth does not fear investigation. Yet the holocaust has been elevated to a special level of importance and has become an almost unquestionable truth as if it were a holy teaching central to a religious cult. Like a religious cult, the industry surrounding the holocaust is so zealous that anyone who dares whisper even the mildest doubt over the authenticity of any detail of the established holocaust narrative is hounded and attacked until they are made an outcast and shunned by the rest of society.

The holocaust, slavery and colonialism have been used as sticks with which to beat Western man and instil within him a sense of guilt and self-hatred. This self-hatred and guilt is expressed most easily in a single word, a word so powerful that it can silence any man, end any debate and once uttered against a man can literally make him a pariah – that word is 'racist'. The word 'racist' is so powerful that grown men cower when it is used as a weapon against them.

The word 'racist' is the modern day equivalent of the word 'witch'. Just as the accusation of being a witch could see an individual face a death sentence, today the accusation of being a 'racist' can cause an individual to lose their job, lead to their incarceration in prison and ultimately isolate them and leave them as an outcast from society. But just like with the accusation of being a witch, there is very little defence one can use when accused of being a racist other than to grovel, creep and beg in the most craven manner.

The word 'racist' has turned Western man into a creature that can only be equated with a whipped dog. On the cry of that one word Western man rolls over and begs for mercy – just as an abused animal would. White guilt, self-hatred and the word 'racist' have been used to break the Western heart and subdue Western bravery and courage in order to prevent Western man from standing up in the defence of his own people. Western man is now so cowed that he dare not speak out against any foreign enemy or threat to his people for fear of being branded a 'racist'.

There is no better example of this than in the northern town of Rotherham. Over 1400 Western girls were systematically groomed, sexually assaulted and raped by Muslim men who were overwhelmingly of foreign descent. Let's look at this horrendous series of acts and examine them in more detail – and ask what was truly shocking about these horrendous crimes.

Was it truly shocking that gangs of Muslim men sought to exploit Western females? The answer is no. When looking at the treatment of women in Islamic countries – especially the treatment of female non-believers – sexual abuse is often common. What's more, the grooming of Western girls by Muslim men had been known about for roughly a decade before the grooming of Western girls in Rotherham made national headlines. The actions of these men, whilst sickening, should not have come as a shock to anyone.

Was it truly shocking that these acts were covered up by the local establishment – politicians and the police? Again the answer is no. It is of no surprise that those motivated by greed – whether it be greed for political power or monetary gain – should cover up vile acts in order to personally profit. Throughout history powerful individuals and groups have covered up criminality and wrongdoing for personal gain. The police officers and politicians who played a part in covering up the grooming of young girls in Rotherham are despicable and should all have been tried for their complicity in these crimes. But the fact that the police and the political establishment were complicit in such crimes should shock no one.

What is truly shocking is that the local community whose daughters were being preyed upon did nothing. The truly jaw-dropping fact that underlies this whole sorry tale is that the local community stood by and let this sickening abuse continue. Grown men chose to watch in silence as their daughters were taken away to be sexually abused, rather than run the risk of being called a 'racist' for speaking out or fighting back, and defending their loved ones.

Make no mistake – the most sickening aspect of the scandal in Rotherham was that no one stood up to what was happening. The community never came together to defend their daughters. Fathers never put up a fight against the men who called at their homes after dark with the intention of abusing their children. What's more, the people of Rotherham did not turn on the police nor did they string up the politicians who were complicit in covering up these crimes – in fact they voted them back into power.

The descendants of the men who died at Thermopylae, who defended the Gates of Vienna and who stood firm at Rorke's Drift simply stood and watched their daughters being taken away by foreign men to be sexually abused; Western man chose to let his daughters be raped rather than risk being called a racist. This is the breaking of the Western heart and the destruction of Western bravery and courage; Western man is now a whipped dog racked with guilt and self-loathing and can be brought to his knees with the use of mere words.

The bravery and courage that Western man was famed for, and that held the world in awe, is now a thing of the past. Western folk have become conditioned to hate themselves through an onslaught of material created to instil guilt in those who view it. Through the bending and manipulation of history Western youngsters have been taught to hate and despise their own ancestors and reject their own culture and heritage.

Western man now walks with his head bowed. He fears speaking his mind and is kept in line not by the rod or the stick but by words like 'racist' and feelings of false guilt that have been forced upon him. Just as Western man has been enslaved by ideals implanted in his own mind, just as Western man poisons his own body by choice – Western man also is in effect his own warden, regulating his own speech and actions in order to ensure he does not break the rules imposed on him by his mortal enemies.

As Europe becomes ever more multicultural, as different cultures vie for power and position within Western cities and towns, conflict will naturally arise. Western man will increasingly be the loser in these conflicts as he now lacks the ability to defend himself, his loved ones and his community. Western man is now so conditioned that he would rather roll over and die than defend himself and risk being called a 'racist'.

Western man is a shadow of his former self: his mind enslaved, his body weakened, his spirit corrupted and the courage and bravery he once possessed radically diminished. The enemies of the West have ripped out the very heart of Western man and left him at the mercy of any foreign foe that chooses to see him and his family as worthy prey.

18
THE RISE OF THE CULT OF INDIVIDUALISM

Western man is a titan and his great achievements and the civilisation he created once held the world in awe. But none of those achievements nor the great civilisation Western man built would have been possible without Western man working together with his brothers and sisters and forming communities, tribes and nations which pulled together for the greater good and which became more than the sum of their individual parts.

Western man changed the world and virtually every single world-altering invention or discovery came from his fertile mind and was developed, industrialised and put into practice by his hand. None of this would have been possible without Western society pulling together and working as one in order to turn great thoughts and plans into great realities.

Take as an example the great works of architecture that fill Western cities. Some of these wonders such as the Colosseum in Rome were built thousands of years ago – yet they are still a cause for inspiration and wonderment even today. It is true that the plans for these great structures were often the visions and designs of an individual architect or a small group of talented designers. However the reason the architects and designers realised their plans is because the cohesive society that surrounded them pulled together in order to turn their plans into magnificent realities.

Just like a colony of bees, when humans come together and form a community that can be likened to a single living and breathing entity, with its own shared consciousness, then what can be achieved is almost limitless and infinitely greater than what can be achieved by mere individuals. The enemies of the West know this – and that is why they have done everything they can to undermine Western society in the numerous ways that have been explained in detail over the course of this book.

The enemies of Western man have used every devious trick they could think of in order to promote the importance of being an individual. They push the notion that individualism should be held up as the highest and most noble virtue. These people scorn the idea of the need for a set of societal standards which allow people to identify with one another and come together as a cohesive community. In fact individualism has become like a cult within Western society. Western man now competes with his brothers and sisters in order to emphasise his own individuality and prove how different he is from those around him.

The cult of individualism affects every aspect of Western life – from the way people dress to the way they style their hair and present themselves. Over time individuals have taken increasingly extreme steps in order to ensure they are truly one of a kind. People now modify their own bodies in ever more outlandish ways in an effort to stand out from the crowd. But the embrace of individualism has a hugely adverse effect on Western society causing it to become less homogenous – rather than a cohesive community, Western society becomes a loose collection of individuals who no longer relate to one another.

Let us now return to the analogy of the bees.

The beehive works because the bees that inhabit the hive are a homogenous group and form a colony. The bees not only look alike but they think alike. The bees have a shared consciousness and work together in harmony for the good of the colony. The bees do not put the good of the individual before the good of the colony, as fundamentally when the good of the colony comes first the colony becomes strong and healthy, and a strong and healthy colony shelters and protects the individual bees. The individual bee does not reason like a human, but on an instinctive and primeval level the bee knows that his individual well-being is tied to the well-being of the colony. Now imagine what would happen to the colony if each and every bee decided to go it alone and push for its own individuality and personal freedoms and put those before the good of the colony. The bees would no longer wish to dance in the same manner; they would no longer be able to communicate effectively with each other and they would become increasingly isolated from one another. As the colony inevitably broke up, the hive itself would crumble and everything the bees had built and strived for would be lost.

Again this analogy may seem simplistic but it illustrates an important point and one that can be directly applied to Western nations. The West was at its strongest when its community was at its most cohesive – and the enemies of Western man know this. That is why once the structures and safeguards that held the West together were weakened, the enemies of the West put into place the final and most devastating part of their plan; to ensure not only the break-up of Western society, but that Western society can never be put back together again.

It is one thing to break up a community – but that process can often be reversed. Times of struggle and hardship can pull a group of people together and cause them to work as one again, forcing them to rediscover common bonds and reunite as a community. However if the individuals that once made up that community had become so different and so disparate that they could no longer relate to one another, then even in times of hardship they would be unable to reunite and work as a cohesive group.

What would make all of this worse is if the people that made up that community no longer interacted with one another or spent time together – instead choosing solitary pursuits which increased their sense of isolation. Imagine if people just sat in front of their television or their computer spending hours watching programmes, playing games and browsing social networks. Not only would the people who made up that once strong community be unable to relate to one another due to their embrace of individualism, but they would no longer have the social skills necessary to interact with one another due to their increasingly solitary and isolated lifestyle.

Think back to maybe fifty or sixty years ago, when families knew everyone who lived on their street. They would know the names of their neighbours, the names of their neighbours' children and where their neighbours worked. What's more they would interact with their neighbours at the local pub, church and at community events. People related to one another – they looked the same, went to the same church, the same pub and their children went to the same schools. Today how many people even know the names of their immediate neighbours who live next door?

One of the ways the cult of individualism has been created is by the introduction of different subcultures into society. These subcultures are pushed through the very same channels as the majority of the other highly damaging material that is aimed at destroying Western society. One of the key ways subcultures form is around music. Subcultures are not just a hobby or a pastime – that is an important distinction. Subcultures are not just something that one indulges in during their spare time, but instead something that are more akin to a way of life.

Subcultures influence the way people dress, the way they talk, the music they listen to, the symbols they identify with and even the very lifestyle they lead. This is not the same as a hobby or a pastime. If someone chooses to go fishing at the weekend, they may wear special clothing – but that clothing is only worn for the duration of the fishing trip. A fisherman doesn't choose to wear those special clothes at all other times to demonstrate to the world that he spends his free time catching fish or so other fishermen can identify with him.

The idea that a fisherman would walk down the high street wearing waders and a fly hat so that other fishermen could identify him is comical. Yet this is exactly what members of subcultures do – members of a particular subculture will ensure they all dress in a similar manner and adopt the same symbols and patches in order to look alike. However on the flip side of the coin, adopting those visual cues ensures that members of a subculture don't look like or identify with those within society who are not a part of their particular subculture.

Imagine a society full of different subcultures – each with their own different way of dressing, talking, their own symbols and their own micro-culture. Society would no longer be a cohesive body; it would instead be made up of a loose group of different subcultures that could be likened to tribes. These tribes would often view each other not only as different, but also with a degree of contempt or even dislike, hence the existence of different subcultures would lead to a fracturing of society.

But you don't have to imagine this scenario – it is another reality faced by the West. Just take a look at the different musical subcultures that exist within society: goths, rockers, punks, headbangers, ravers and mods to name just a few. One could spend an entire day listing the different musical subcultures and the different ways each group has of 'standing out' from the crowd. The people pushing this divisive nonsense are the enemies of the West and again you can trace this attack back to its roots and see when it began. Let's look at the mods and rockers.

The mods and rockers were two conflicting musical subcultures that came to prominence in the 1960s and 1970s. The rocker subculture was centred on motorcycling, and their appearance reflected that. Rockers generally wore motorcycle style clothing such as black leather jackets and boots. The mod subculture was centred on scooters and mods wore suits and other clean-cut outfits.

It was not enough that the adoption of these subcultures led to a visible schism in society that served to divide Western youth – but the adoption of such subcultures also led to violence. Mods and rockers would regularly fight each other. These fights were not fought over national sovereignty or the continued existence of one's people, in fact these fights were not fought for any noble cause. The battles between the mods and the rockers took place for no other reason than the fact that mods and rockers were different. Riots took place between mods and rockers at different seaside resorts and the violence escalated to include the use of knives and other weapons.

Essentially two different factions of Western youth were formed and both hated one another without any valid reason. These factions fought bitter and violent battles – again for no reason. This schism in society was not a natural occurrence but was manufactured by the enemies of the West in an attempt to divide and conquer Western man. The creation of these subcultures is another attack on Western civilisation. As with the other attacks on Western man, this attack was pushed through the media, the music industry and by the bad role models that are foisted upon young and impressionable Western minds.

Today the mods and the rockers aren't the dominant subcultures – there are so many different subcultures it would be impossible to pick one as dominant. Rather than being one large and cohesive community, Western youth is fractured into hundreds of different groups each with their own ways. Each subculture is different enough to ensure that the small numbers attached to it identify more closely with their own tiny group than with the rest of society.

Rockers are now split into separate smaller subcultures that listen to punk, heavy metal, rock, thrash metal, black metal and numerous other musical offshoots of the original genre. As these subcultures become smaller and more diverse there is an ever increasing push for a greater degree of individuality. As new subcultures emerge youngsters are drawn to them in order to stand out from the crowd and assert their own individuality. Often within these subcultures a type of anarchy is favoured to ensure each individual within the group is different to his or her companions.

Instead of subcultures becoming larger and more cohesive over time the trend is the opposite. Over time larger subcultures fracture and an increasing number of smaller subcultures are created, and each of these smaller subcultures then attempts to differentiate itself from the pack and assert its own uniqueness. This has the obvious effect of tearing society apart and creating differences where there used to be uniformity.

Now imagine this trend pushed to its logical extreme – the ultimate form of differentiation, a gang of one, an individual who is completely unique and totally different from everyone else in society and stands as an island unto himself. This is obviously the end game of this devious plan and can be seen in the way people dress, the way they present themselves, the colour of their hair and of course through body modifications such as tattoos, piercings and much more outlandish and degenerate transformations that individuals now commit to.

Individuals now do anything and everything they can to stand out from the crowd. You only have to walk down the high street to see a thousand different fashions, haircuts and body modifications. No two people look alike and even those within the same subculture do everything they can to stand out from their own group. As time goes by the modifications people undergo to make themselves stand out become ever more degenerate and outlandish – stretched ears, dermal implants, full face tattoos, split tongues, tattooed eyeballs and now even artificial horns implanted on their skulls!

But what is the root cause of people embracing these crazy fashions, haircuts and body modifications? At the heart of this drive for individuality is a childlike form of attention seeking. The people trying to stand out from the crowd by pursuing these ways of life and embracing these fads are effectively screaming 'look at me'. Why does the naughty child throw a tantrum or hurl his food across the table at his parents? The answer is simple; the naughty child 'plays up' in an attempt to gain attention from his parents in order to feel like he is the centre of proceedings.

This basic drive for attention is something we are born with and serves us well as babies. When we are a tiny infant one of the most basic and natural behavioural patterns we are gifted with is to scream and cry when we need attention – as attention brings the parental figure (usually the mother) to tend to whatever need is currently wanting. For example, when a baby wants to eat, he or she cannot simply ask calmly for food, nor can he or she provide the food for themselves, so by crying this brings the attention of the parental figure who then satisfies the need of the child.

This is one of the first and most important lessons a child learns – by making a scene they stand out and gain attention which brings them satisfaction. However as a child grows up and develops and the parents impart morals and learned behaviour to the child, the child learns not to scream and shout and play up, but to ask for what he or she desires, and if brought up correctly that child also learns to accept when he or she cannot immediately have what they desire.

The process of developing a healthy superego involves growing out of behaving like a child; the developed superego scorns attention seeking on a childlike level. When a child is seen screaming and crying and throwing a tantrum in a public place, that child is seeking attention and is clearly the product of poor parenting. It is crucial to understand that when a child throws public tantrums it is a sign that the child is not mentally developing as it should; the child's id is still ruling its psyche and the id seeks immediate gratification through attention seeking on an undeveloped level as a newborn baby would.

When a helpless infant cries for attention, the attention that is forthcoming makes the infant feel good and the infant makes an association between gaining attention and the feeling of satisfaction. If this desire for attention is not removed as the child grows older – if the child does not develop a functioning superego – then the adult will still seek attention in a childlike way. Whilst grown adults rarely seek attention by throwing tantrums, they now embrace individuality so they can stand out from the crowd in order to ensure everyone looks at them and gives them the attention they crave.

By dying their hair bright pink, by shaving half of their head, by wearing ludicrous or revealing clothing, by sporting a large and visible set of tattoos or by modifying their body in some debased tribal manner – the individual is crying 'look at me'. The individual seeks attention from other people in order to satisfy their id in the same way the child seeks to satisfy the id when it throws a tantrum in the middle of a supermarket or shopping centre.

The problem faced by Western man is that not only are more and more people seeking this attention through the cult of individualism, but also that the cult of individualism is a self-perpetuating and accelerating phenomenon. Just as the enemies of the West have pushed the envelope of degeneracy in film and music, they seek to push forward the cult of individualism. The cult of individualism has gathered momentum like a snowball rolling down a hill.

What makes one person stand out from the crowd today is relatively passé tomorrow. At one time a man with an earring would have garnered curious looks; today no one would blink an eyelid. So instead people now stretch their ears like an African tribesman and insert huge hoops through the skin of their ear lobes. But now that the stretched ear is becoming more common, the 'trendsetters' seek to stand out and stretch their noses, cheeks, lips and even have these 'flesh tunnels' inserted in other places in an effort to be unique and gain the maximum attention possible from those around them.

This is of course perpetuated further by social networks such as Facebook which are under the control of the enemies of the West. People now use these social networks to create as much outrage and controversy as possible by posting 'selfies' of their outrageous 'styles'. Of course the entire selfie culture is simply attention seeking at its worst – but when everyone is doing it the individual seeks increasingly crazy ways to make their selfie stand out from the crowd in order to attain more of the attention they crave.

Like children rolling around wailing in the aisle of a supermarket, the grown adult now seeks to satiate the call of their id by ensuring that everyone looks at them. This makes the individual feel special and wanted – just like the child does when their parent picks them up off the floor and hugs them. The enemies of the West have damaged and undermined the superego by altering the conditions that allow the superego to develop. This has left adults being ruled by their id and one of the most damaging consequences of this is the development of the cult of individualism which is both childish in its nature and detrimental to the cohesiveness of Western society.

As the cult of individualism reaches an insane peak with ever more people joining in the cry for attention, the creatures this cult creates become ever more insane and debased. Young people write blogs claiming that they are in fact animals trapped in human bodies. Grown men wear children's nappies and roll around in their own faeces. Youngsters get outrageous body art and modifications which permanently alter their appearance. Confused individuals demand sex changes and mutilate their genitals. But the driving force behind all of this madness is the childlike craving for attention.

Western man is being pulled in a hundred or more different directions. The individual attempts to stand out from the crowd and embraces individualism in an increasingly outlandish manner. The homogenous Western society where people looked alike, acted alike and thought along the same lines is now gone, shattered into a million pieces. But a greater problem lies in the task of putting those pieces back together, as the process of fixing this mess is made all the more difficult as the pieces that once made up Western society are now so different they no longer fit together as they should.

As a result Western man will be placed at a huge disadvantage if he is ever threatened by a strong and cohesive foreign culture that acts as single entity. The disparate nature of Western society will prevent Western man from launching an effective defence. How on earth are a group of people meant to ever come together and act as a cohesive society if every single person is doing everything they can to be as different to the next person as humanly possible? Think back to what makes the perfect society:

The perfect society can be defined as a group of people who come together with shared morals, shared values and wish to move forward as one, working together for the good of the community whilst not forgetting the

rights and importance of the individual. This community cohesion relies on a shared sense of consciousness held by the people who make up that society.

But people are now drifting apart; they no longer share the same morals, and rather than grouping together, they identify with and chose to be around ever smaller and increasingly differentiated subcultures. The sense of community consciousness in the West has been destroyed and tiny groups seek to better themselves and look out for their own interests over and above the interests of society.

Western man has embraced the cult of individualism. Western man's desire and drive to be as unique as possible has led to the fracturing of Western society. The drive for uniqueness has had an adverse effect on the common bonds within Western society causing those bonds to weaken. The common traditions, culture, dress and appearance that made Western society homogenous have now been abandoned in favour of individualism.

The enemies of the West have played a devious and divisive game that has undermined the common values and homogeneity found within Western society. Sadly this places Western man at the mercy of other races and cultures who have settled in the West yet retained their traditions and values and remained as singular cohesive communities.

19
THE DEATH OF THE WESTERN SUPEREGO

The enemies of the West seek to destroy Western man and plunge Western civilisation into a state of madness and degeneracy from which it will never recover. The enemies of the West are 'nation wreckers' that seek to undermine the sovereignty of nations and states in order to make them weak so they can plunder their wealth and enrich themselves through the misery of others. But in order to defeat Western man and reduce Western civilisation to ash, the enemies of the West must first destroy the essence of Western man.

The Western superego is the essence of Western man and it is this essence that the enemies of the West seek to destroy, for when that essence is extinguished Western man will no longer possess the characteristics that made him great.

The superego is of course the learned part of the psyche, the morals, the values and the very traditions that are passed down from generation to generation that mould young minds into dependable and upstanding adults. When a group of people share the same traditions and have a shared sense of moral values, they pass down those shared characteristics to their offspring. Everyone in that group grows up surrounded by others who share the same community logic which allows the group to form a community consciousness.

The Western superego is the embodiment of Western man's community consciousness. The Western superego has been evolving and developing for over 40,000 years since early Western man existed on the edge of Northern Europe's ice sheets and hunted animals that are now long extinct. Western man has passed down his DNA from generation to generation and that has ensured that his physical traits have survived and been strengthened. Western man has also passed down the Western superego through lessons and teachings.

By passing down learned morality and values from generation to generation, Western man has ensured that it is not only his DNA that lives on in future generations. Western man has ensured that his mentality and ways of thinking live on by passing down his superego to his offspring. This ensures that not only do

Western man's physical traits live on, but in a very real way his soul also lives on through future generations.

Just as the DNA of Western man has changed and evolved over time to favour stronger genetic traits, the Western superego evolved over time to favour stronger morals and values that have acted as the glue that held communities and families together. It became a selective pressure to stick with your own and to be loyal to your family and tribe – this was bred into Western man and reinforced and strengthened through imparting these values again and again to future generations. Over many thousands and thousands of years the Western superego developed and changed and it was not only values that were passed down but also traditions and ways of life.

As Western man advanced and civilisation grew, so did the Western superego; it was no longer simply a set of binding moral values, but now embodied traditions that stretched back over millennia that became a rich culture. The Western superego consists of the values, morals and traditions of Western man – the very essence of what makes Western man who he is, and the very stuff that binds Western man to his brothers and sisters and creates a community that works as one cohesive group.

The morals, values and traditions that were passed down from generation to generation slowly evolved into a rich culture that was expressed through language, art, song, dress and architecture. These expressions of Western culture gave rise to a rich heritage that stretches back for millennia and which has left lasting footprints in the sands of time – footprints that show current generations just where their ancestors have come from and the path their ancestors had taken.

What's more, those footprints in the sands of time not only showed future generations where their ancestors had come from, but they acted as a road map that pointed future generations in the right direction. Those footprints helped mark the way so that as civilisation developed, future generations could see the correct path to take. But importantly a strong community-wide superego not only points out the correct path, but it also causes a community to walk that path together and work as a singular unit. A community or a nation is only strong when the people it consists of work as one and pull together in the same direction.

When a nation works together as a cohesive group that nation advances and has a far greater chance of warding off threats. But once a nation begins to fracture and divisions appear, the community becomes disparate and is no longer a community but a collection of individuals that no longer relate to one another and as a result begin pulling in different directions. The enemies of the West know this and to conquer Western man they set about attacking the Western superego with the aim of destroying the bonds that hold Western society together.

We will return to the case of the beehive:

Bees produce honey – and honey is delicious and highly sought after both by man and beast alike. Honey has a high nutrient value and is a wonderful natural food source. But to get honey is no easy feat as the honey is stored deep within the hive and is protected by an entire army of bees. Once the hive is under attack the entire colony will mount an aggressive defence. It would be easy to simply state that the strength of the hive's defence lies merely in the overwhelming number of bees that will emerge to oppose any would-be thieves.

However to simply think that numbers are all that matter is to miss the fundamental issue which is in fact the selfless dedication of the individual to the colony. When a hostile intruder attempts to take the life source of the colony that intruder is met with an overwhelming response, but that overwhelming response comes from many individual bees acting as one.

The unfortunate truth that comes with any defence of the hive is that many individual bees will in fact perish. Bees are unfortunate in that when they attack and sting an enemy, it seals their own fate – every successful sting results in the death of the bee that landed the blow. The bee therefore literally puts the good of the colony before its own life; the bee gives everything in order to ensure the colony survives. The whole defence of the colony is mounted on the pretext of the greater good.

This way of thinking is what has ensured the long-term survival of bees as a species, as it has protected countless colonies and put off many would-be attackers who eyed the honey as a prized meal. What could be more devastating or more painful than to be stung hundreds or thousands of times all over your body? What could be a greater deterrent to those who would happily seek the honey that belongs rightfully to the bees?

A head-on assault would be almost suicidal – or at least very painful. But imagine attacking a hive where each bee thought of itself above the interests of the colony, where each bee was an individual who didn't connect with the other bees that surrounded it. Imagine a beehive where, if an attacker chose to attempt to plunder the honey, the bees thought of themselves before they thought of the colony and either hid in the hive or flew away to ensure their own safety. That hive would be plundered and ultimately the bees would be driven to extinction. If the community consciousness of the hive is destroyed the bees would be done for.

It is no different within the world of man. Civilisations and nations only survive when the people who make up those civilisations and nations stick together and work as one in order to repel their enemies and stand strong in the face of adversity. It is the sense of community that holds people together, a sense of the greater good that comes from common bonds. That common bond for Western man is the Western superego. That is why the enemies of the West have set about to attack the Western superego.

To undermine the will of a nation to work as one group and to prevent individuals working together for the greater good of society is to seal the fate of that nation. If Western man hadn't been so selfless in the defence of his people and his land, if Western man hadn't put the greater good of his nation before himself, the Western world would have ceased to exist a long time ago. It is this community spirit that has seen Western man weather so many storms and triumph again and again even in the face of overwhelming odds.

The enemies of the West have a strong grasp of history and they are certainly not fools; they know that to defeat Western man it is no good to simply mount a head-on assault on the West. To defeat Western man, first and foremost the essence of Western man must be broken.

This attack on the Western superego has been carefully orchestrated through numerous means that have been discussed at great length. The aims of these attacks are to prevent the older generation and the younger generation identifying with one another – essentially creating a generation gap. The generation gap prevents the older generation from passing down the superego to the younger generation, and prevents the morals, values and traditions of that society being passed down.

As this generation gap prevents the passing down of morals, values and traditions, the very culture that was central to Western society begins to fade. Once the young in any society no longer look to their ancestors and no longer seek to follow the footprints previous generations have left in the sand, those generations end up going off track and become lost. A strong culture binds a group of people together and is like the glue that holds society together. When the young no longer follow a strong culture and become lost, they are easy prey for those who wish to lead them further astray.

Creating the generation gap allows the younger and more impressionable within society to be more easily manipulated by the enemies of the West. The younger and more impressionable within society are easily led astray and can be taken down an ever more destructive path once they have been separated from their elders who they should be listening to and attempting to emulate. Once this has been achieved, traditions, morals and values are lost and false morality and degeneracy can then be implanted into the minds of those who have been led astray.

When traditions are no longer passed down they are forgotten and become relics of the past that are viewed as 'quirky' and 'old-fashioned'. The few that continue to uphold such traditions are then painted as 'odd' and 'out-of-touch'. The traditions that have served Western man well for thousands of years are then confined to the dustbin of history within a few short decades. This represents the death of Western culture.

Once Western culture has been destroyed and Western man has been separated from the traditions that link him to his ancestors and the ways of the past, a vacuum is then created. That vacuum is then filled – not by positive values, not by morality and not by anything wholesome. The vacuum created when Western man loses his culture is always filled by negatives that are promoted by the enemies of the West. What was once a healthy and moral culture is replaced by a degenerate and debased counterculture.

Whereas traditional Western culture was linked to the past and laid out a road map that stretched back for millennia and pointed Western man in a positive and healthy direction, the counterculture points to many different but equally fruitless dead ends. The death of Western culture created a vacuum, and that vacuum has been filled by the counterculture which was created to lead Western man away from the path his ancestors took and down a road that ends with the demise of Western man.

Traditional Western culture enshrined positive virtues that were emphasised in order to keep society on track and headed in the right direction. Western culture kept the mind, body, heart and soul healthy and fulfilled. Western man, through his own traditions, was taught that at the centre of his world should be blood, soil and spirituality. However the counterculture is a wholly negative invention that has been used to fill the vacuum created by the lack of genuine culture with something insidious.

The counterculture created by the enemies of the West is not aimed at holding Western society together. The focus of the counterculture is not family bonds or national pride. The counterculture causes Western man to seek short-term hedonistic pleasure and embrace his animalistic instincts and pursue instant gratification. Western man no longer looks to the examples set by his ancestors, but looks to false role models held up by his enemies with the intention of implanting poor morals and values into Western minds. These role models seek to emphasise everything that Western man should not embrace – immorality and valueless nonsense is the message they impart.

The false role models foisted upon Western man push everything that lacks moral substance and everything that is degenerate. These role models tell Western man that short-term gain is more important than long-term goals and thus that Western man should always give in to his animal instincts in order to attain the instant gratification his id desires. Once this short termism is embraced, it leads to gluttony, greed, lust and laziness ruling the mind of Western man. Once such dubious virtues are embraced, the outward manifestations of this poison are clear to see.

Every single healthy trait that once defined Western society slowly withers and is replaced by materialism, obesity, drug abuse, sexual debauchery and even a hatred for one's self and one's ancestors and the historical achievements of those ancestors. As these unhealthy obsessions firmly take root in the hearts and minds of Western man, the natural and healthy culture of old becomes less and less attractive as it emphasises a morality that doesn't stand for instant gratification.

This transformation from culture to counterculture can be seen quite simply as the regression of man from a highly evolved and mentally adept creature with a strong sense of self control and duty to a pleasure-driven animal governed by selfish desires. This is the death of the Western superego – it is the death of Western culture itself, and with it comes the rise of the id and the drive for unending individualistic and animalistic pleasure.

Regression is the perfect word to describe this phenomenon. As humans we are closer to animals when we are first born as our only instincts are the natural drives for pleasure, and satisfying those pleasures is our only goal. As an individual grows and develops and as the superego is implanted in the individual's psyche by its parents, the individual progresses and learns to control and temper its natural instincts and behave within an adult and moral framework. This framework and adult reasoning is what allows society to function. Once that framework is removed and the individual throws off culture and embraces the counterculture, that individual begins regressing to a lower state – mentally the individual starts becoming more and more childlike.

This childlike state that now rules the Western mind sees Western man seeking attention as an infant would, through the embrace of individualism as Western man cries out to be looked at and acknowledged. This childlike craving is no different than a toddler throwing a tantrum and crying for everyone around it to stare and look at its ill-behaved antics. But to gain attention today, in a world where every natural barrier has been broken down, is an increasingly difficult task. The individual must go to increasingly outlandish lengths in order to be different.

As the regressing mind craves attention, it will go to ever greater lengths for acknowledgment, meaning that each and every person tries to push the envelope of individualism as far as they can in whichever direction they so favour. Instead of coming together and following the path laid out by his ancestors, Western man is fractured and running in so many different and opposite directions that society is no longer cohesive and cannot be described as a community.

Western man no longer looks like his brothers and sisters. Western man styles himself in ways that are more akin to a debased and primitive tribesman, and embraces odd and destructive subcultures in a race to be different and garner as much attention as possible. Western man seeks out pleasures that not only damage him as an individual, but these pleasures further pull and tear apart what is left of Western society. These pleasures come before family, folk and soil and serve to satisfy only selfish desires.

When Western man was part of a cohesive community, the achievements of that community were so magnificent they not only shaped the development of the West, but the development of the whole world. These achievements spanned every imaginable sphere of knowledge and art – architecture, poetry, literature, song, dance, fine painting, engineering, physics, chemistry and industrial growth.

Great achievements like the Colosseum in Rome, the ancient aqueducts and castles of Northern Europe, still put to shame what most other cultures have achieved to this day. The writings of Shakespeare and Homer, the poetry of Keats, the beautiful art of Michelangelo, Leonardo and Turner all still inspire the world to this day and are largely unmatched. Inventions like alternating current, the combustion engine and medical advances like vaccinations changed the whole world.

All of these achievements sprung forth from Western man, but all of these achievements were only possible because of the strong community that pulled together in order to make the dreams and ideas of exceptional individuals into realities. What's more, protecting these achievements and guarding them from would-be conquerors was also only possible because Western man stood together as a community.

The death of the Western superego is not just the death of the Western community, and it is not just the death of Western nations. The death of the Western superego is the death of the very spirit that made possible the great achievements that have defined the West and shaped the development of the whole world. The death of the Western superego will not only spell the end for Western man – but will also see all the great achievements of Western man's ancestors crumble and be lost to the mists of time.

In a very real sense, the death of the Western superego means the death and destruction of a lineage that stretches back for millennia and encompasses the greatest achievements the world has ever known. If Western man allows this, then Western man not only dooms himself, but in his own death he seals the fate of all those who came before him and renders their great achievements and sacrifices meaningless. If the Western superego perishes, then all that has ever gone before will have been for nought.

Once the Western superego has been destroyed, Western man will be exactly as the enemies of the West wish him to be – a childlike and base creature that simply lives for pleasure. The death of the Western superego will give rise to the triumph of the id and the death of all of Western civilisation.

20

THE TRIUMPH OF THE ID AND THE DEATH OF THE WEST

The death of the Western superego precedes the fall of Western man and the destruction of Western civilisation itself. The period we are now living in can be described as the end times for Western civilisation and the next few generations of Western man will bear witness to the death of the West. The conditions for a perfect storm are now in place and in that storm the West will be washed away and consigned to the history books – if indeed history books are ever written again in the absence of Western man.

The death of the West will not come about in one magnificent yet tragic final battle that eclipses all others that have gone before it. The death of the West will not occur in some 'race war' or in a series of great conflicts where battle lines are clearly drawn and armies clash in a final epic military engagement. The death of the West will be a creeping one – like a cancer that eats away at an organism, slowly weakening the suffering creature over a long period of time. The death of the West will be akin to a death of a thousand cuts rather than one significant blow.

Many have theorised that eventually immigrants that have come to settle in the West and whose communities have grown in size will one day turn on Western man – that foreign communities will form a fifth column within the West and initiate a great conflict on Western soil. This theory surmises a racial or religious conflict on a grand scale between Western man and those immigrants who have come to settle in the West yet retained a culture that is hostile to that of Western culture.

This theory of a great war is not only misguided, but is also highly damaging to the cause of saving Western man. It relies on the idea that Western man is who he once was and that he still has his mind, body, soul and heart intact. The idea of a great racial or religious war – and one where Western man would be victorious – is actually laughable. This war will never take place, but instead the death of the West will take place house by house, street by street, town by town and city by city, like a creeping shroud falling over Western nations.

Let's stop for one minute and actually analyse the theory behind the idea of a racial or religious conflict on the level some theorise – what's more, let's look at the likely outcome if such a war was to take place. For a giant conflict to engulf a nation, battle lines must first form and for this to occur different homogenous groups must exist. Homogenous groups form based on common bonds between the people who make up those groups.

Therein lies the first major problem with the idea of a racial or religious war – whilst the different cultures and races that have emigrated to the West have retained their group consciousness, Western man has not. If there was a racial or religious conflict the individuals within homogenous communities would come together to protect their own community, but sadly Western man would be unlikely to come together with his brothers and sisters and would be unable to form a single homogenous group. The drive for individuality and isolation that has been pushed upon Western man by the enemies of the West has robbed Western man of the common bonds that once bound Western society together.

Western man no longer has the common cultural bonds, traditions and moral values that once bound him to his brothers and sisters. Western society is no longer homogenous and cohesive; Western society is a loose-knit group of individuals who no longer relate to each other. The subcultures that have sprung up and been embraced so enthusiastically by Western man have driven him into ever smaller groups which no longer relate to one another.

Western man used to know his neighbours – in fact he knew everyone on his street and the streets adjacent to where he lived. He worked with his neighbours, drank with his neighbours and went to church with them. Everyone in Western society knew one another and the common bonds they shared held them together as a community. Now many Western folk don't even know the names of those who live next door to them – let alone the names of all those who live on their street. Western man's public houses have closed, his industry has been exported and his churches lay empty.

This is the complete opposite of the situation that can be observed in immigrant communities that have come to settle in the West. The immigrants that have settled in Western nations have formed their own strong and close-knit communities where people know each other, where there are established community leaders who command respect, where entire families live on the same street and where everyone knows the names of their neighbours. The people in these communities look out for one another, do business with one another and worship at the same temples. These communities cherish their traditions and wish to preserve the shared heritage which was passed down by their ancestors and now acts as the glue that holds their community together.

If Western man was forced to come together as a group in order to fight a fifth column within his own nation, how would he fare? The answer is clear – he would be overwhelmed. Western society is a disparate group; a weak collection of individuals – many of these individuals wouldn't even want to stand with one another as they wouldn't know each other and wouldn't be able to relate to one another. On the other hand many immigrant communities would be strong and stand as one. The implications of this do not need explaining in detail.

The second main reason that Western man would not emerge victorious from a civil war based along ethnic or cultural lines is that Western man no longer holds the right priorities in life. Western man is now materialistic, individualistic and hedonistic. Not only would Western man lack the strong community and the group consciousness needed in order to stand a chance of winning a civil war, but Western man would also lack the motivation to fight, for Western man no longer sees value in anything genuinely meaningful or worthwhile.

When great sacrifices are made and great acts of bravery are displayed – such as in the Battle of Vienna – the men who faced such overwhelming odds had strong beliefs that allowed them to override their instinct of individual preservation in order to serve the greater good of their people. When faced with almost certain death the natural drive – provided from the ego (reality principle) – is to flee. However a developed superego can override that instinct and the preservation of the group is put before the preservation of the individual.

The great sacrifices made by Western man throughout history were indicative of his priorities in life. Western man prioritised things that made him spiritually strong – family, folk, faith and soil. Western man had deep connections to his immediate nuclear family, the community in which he lived, his religion and the land that he called home. Now Western man is disconnected from all of these things. The nuclear family has been undermined, the Western community is fractured, religion has either been watered down or forgotten and finally Western man is no longer connected to the natural world around him, instead cocooned in walls of brick and concrete where he stares mindlessly at a variety of flickering screens.

Western man's priorities in life made him strong and gave him good reasons to fight, however his priorities in life have now shifted. Individualism, hedonism and materialism have become the new priorities for Western man – but all of those callings are selfish and are centred on personal pleasure and self-gratification. Feeding those pleasures are the priority, which means in times of conflict Western man would be more likely to flee with as much wealth as he could carry or hide in order to live another day in the hope of continuing to seek personal pleasure at a later date.

Think back to the days of the First World War – the bloodiest and most destructive period of warfare the world has ever known. What motivated Western man to climb up out of his trenches and charge at machine-gun emplacements protected by barbed wire fences? Trench warfare is one of the most brutal types of combat the world has ever known and one that sees enormous numbers of casualties stack up very quickly; in fact offensive manoeuvres were often almost suicidal. Yet what motivated young men to 'go over the top' and face certain death? The brave men who threw themselves into barbed wire fences and were cut down by machine-gun fire were motivated by spiritual priorities which strengthened their resolve and allowed them to override their own natural survival instinct.

These same spiritual callings to folk, faith and family may be lost to Western man – but that doesn't mean they are lost to the immigrant communities that have settled in Western nations. Many of the immigrant communities living in the Western world still form strong families, have lower divorce rates, attend religious institutions regularly and as stated earlier are part of a tight-knit community. These higher spiritual priorities are what motivate people to fight bravely.

The enemies of the West have stripped Western man of his spirituality and damaged the Western soul – replacing Western man's natural callings with warped false idols. But the immigrant communities that have flooded the West have retained their spiritual callings and have continued to prioritise the right things in life. As such if a conflict ever arose, Western man would not be fighting with the fervour of his enemies, but simply trying to live another day in order to carry on his pursuit of individualistic pleasures. By stripping Western man of his reasons to fight, the enemies of the West have pulled a horrible trick: they have left Western man not only isolated, but also left him lacking the inner convictions and motivations that made Western man such a formidable warrior.

Finally and quite crucially, if a racial or religious war did erupt and plunge Western nations into a state of civil war, would Western man even allow himself to take part in a conflict where the battles lines were drawn up based on the ethnicity of the combatants? Western society is fractured; Western man is disparate and individualistic, but Western man is also brainwashed and enslaved by notions of white guilt that stem from false historical narratives of his colonial past, slavery and the holocaust. Western man has had his brave heart subdued out of the fear of being called a 'racist'.

Would Western man have what it takes to actually participate in an ethnic conflict without fearing that he was in some way 'racist' for raising a hand in self-defence? Would Western man simply roll over and die before partaking in a battle where the lines were drawn on racial or religious grounds? Could Western man fight to defend the very people he has been taught to hate? Huge swathes of Western society would actively roll over and die, or worse still, attack the few Western men who sought to come together and defend their families and what was left of their communities.

Some may mock this assertion and claim that 'when the time comes' Western man will 'wake up' and do what is 'necessary'. However those believing that years of media brainwashing will be undone in a single moment, similar to a 'road to Damascus' conversion, are simply delusional. The case of Muslim grooming gangs can again be cited – thousands of young Western girls have been sexually abused by Islamic immigrants, yet for over a decade there was silence on the issue as people feared it was worse to run the risk of being called 'racist' than it was to see Western girls being sexually abused.

Western man is no longer brave and courageous, but is now craven and cowardly. The thought of being 'socially unacceptable' is now more frightening than the reality of having your daughter raped! The absurd notion that a single word could bring a grown man to his knees and have him break down in a fit of protestations and apologies should be laughable – yet this is no laughing matter. As soon as the word 'racist' is used it silences any form of debate or discourse and leaves the accused begging in order for the wider audience to see that he is not 'racist', but in fact 'tolerant' and fully in favour of 'diversity'.

Imagine for a second that a great civil war was about to break out in Western nations and the divides in this war were to be formed on the grounds of ethnicity. If Western man stood up to defend himself he would be accused by his own misguided brothers and sisters of being 'racist'. Sadly these accusations would cause large numbers of Western men to bow their heads and sit down meekly to await their fate, as for some even death is preferable to being branded a racist!

Do not underestimate the ability of the word 'racist' to disarm Western man. There are books written titled 'White Privilege', television shows commissioned called 'White Guilt' where Western folk sit and talk about their horrible feelings of guilt for the 'crimes' of their ancestors, and even marches take place where Western folk chain themselves together like slaves and walk through cities wearing t-shirts proclaiming they are 'so sorry'. Do not underestimate the effect that the prolonged message of white guilt and self-hate has had on the mind of Western man.

Even if you choose to ignore the loss of community, the loss of a reason to fight and the fear of being called 'racist', there is still the issue of Western man's level of physical fitness. Does Western man even have the capacity to fight in a civil war? The answer is probably no. If there ever was a great conflict, how would the flabby and unfit Western man cope? Would he perform admirably on the battlefield, or would he put his junk food to one side, roll off his sofa, turn off the television and emerge from his home in a state that would see him short of breath before he had even faced his foe? Again, this is a question that requires no answer.

So if the death of the West is rapidly approaching, and if the death of the West will not come about through civil strife or war, how will it occur? Quite simply the death of the West will come about through demographic change – it will happen house by house, street by street and town by town. It will be a slow process that accelerates over time until Western man is a minority in his own lands and is finally bred out of existence. This will not be genocide by the sword or by the gun, but genocide through diversity and creeping demographic change.

Hundreds of thousands of immigrants flood Western nations each year. As those immigrants have a much higher birth rate, and because Western man's birth rate is in such shocking decline, the trend is clear. As time goes by Western man will become less dominant within the overall population until eventually he becomes a minority in his own land. It will start with houses in the same streets being slowly bought up by those from the same ethnic group who wish to live close by one another. Then when several streets are all made up of one ethnicity, the area will then slowly transform with shops, community centres and religious buildings being erected to serve the immigrant population. Eventually, as more and more of that ethnic group cluster together and as they have more and more children, it will not just be streets or areas that change, but whole towns and cities.

Of course none of this happens overnight; it is a slow and creeping process and one that is aided by Western man himself. Western man now has fewer children and is increasingly eager to sell up and move away from areas experiencing demographic change. Western man does this in order to escape the issue that surrounds him and pretend it isn't happening – after all to oppose this demographic change would put Western man in jeopardy of being branded a racist! We have already seen that Western man's birth rate has fallen to a low of 1.3, a critical low from which there may well be no coming back.

The ethnic groups coming to the West have a booming population and the sound of their children playing will fill the streets, conversely the sound of the coughs and splutters of Western man will fill retirement homes. The youthful and strong immigrant communities that have been formed in Western cities will grow and flourish, whilst the Western population literally withers and dies. There will be no need for civil conflict or a war that engulfs nations – the war will be won slowly and the West will die a prolonged and undignified death.

By the middle of the 21st century, Western man will no longer be the majority in most Western nations. By that time, the whole political and social landscape in the West will have changed so dramatically that the West will effectively be on its deathbed. Those fantasising over a civil war or wishing for a glorious fightback will no longer be in any position to stage that fightback – the demographic shift will leave Western man as a disparate minority seeking individual safety.

Granted, immigrant communities may well be more brazen when demographics have shifted further in their favour. It is highly likely that Western man will increasingly be the victim of racially or religiously motivated attacks. Western man will most likely bear witness to skirmishes that see what is left of his community being forced out of areas where he has become a minority. What's more, Western man will likely be admonished for not following the religious or cultural rules that have been imposed upon him by the immigrant population. But if Western man is not fighting back against these things now, when he is a majority, he certainly won't be fighting back against them as an aging minority that has experienced decades more of the brainwashing and white guilt pushed by the media.

Western man may well see racially or religiously motivated rioting increase within the towns and cities where he was once a majority. Civil disorder and violence directed against Western man by those from immigrant communities may well also increase over time. What's more, the rioting and civil disorder may well last for days or even weeks at a time. There may be cases where Western man forms small pockets of resistance against such violence. But without an organised community, without shared morals, without deeper and spiritually meaningful priorities there will be no organised nationwide fightback. What's more, anyone planning such a fightback will have the spectre of the word 'racist' hanging over them.

As this all unfolds – as the madness reaches a crescendo and the decay of Western civilisation accelerates – what of Western man, what will become of him? As things get worse – which they inevitably will, as cities and towns become foreign places and Western man becomes a stranger in his own land – most Western folk won't even notice. Western man will be too busy partying, consuming and cocooning himself in his own private world. Western man will fiddle as 'Rome burns'.

With the death of the Western superego comes the unleashing of the id. Without a developed superego in place – and without a community-wide consciousness – Western man will be reduced to a creature that simply follows its most base instincts. As the West crumbles, and as Western man becomes a minority, he will be too busy gorging on junk food, abusing alcohol and drugs, partying in nightclubs, having promiscuous sex and pursuing every kind of hedonistic pursuit one can imagine. Without a developed superego to keep the id in check, Western man will merely be a beast driven by the pleasure principle.

Not only will Western man not notice what is going on around him – he will not even care if it is pointed out. The only drives Western man will wish to satisfy are those of personal self-indulgent pleasure: Western man will not care for protecting his community and looking out for his brothers and sisters. As the West finally sinks, the look on the face of Western man will not be one of horror, but one of insane mirth as he dances toward his demise. The id will have truly triumphed and that triumph signals the fall of Western man and end of the West.

However all is not yet lost. Western man may well be on the brink of extinction, but whilst Western man still clings on, there is a glimmer of hope and the chance of redemption. But as the enemies of the West have done everything they can to break Western man and damage his psyche, they have also placed false salvation in front of him. The enemies of the West are clever and resourceful; they know that their plan is not without flaws and they know that Western man is a formidable foe.

But whilst there is false salvation and controlled opposition to the enemies of the West, there is also real hope and true salvation. Western man's true salvation lies in reclaiming what made him great and rediscovering the Western superego and resurrecting it in its true form. Before that can be done, first the false salvation that has been deviously created and controlled by the enemies of the West must be exposed and put to rest.

To move forward Western man must walk down the correct path – not the paths laid out by his enemies that will lead him to dead ends and eventual extinction.

21
FALSE SALVATION – CONSERVATISM

When an individual begins to wake up and see that Western society is headed down the wrong path, that individual will naturally seek answers as to why this is the case. In their quest for knowledge, and eventually in their desire to combat the problems they see around them, they will often turn to conservatism. Conservatism is a political and social philosophy that promotes retaining traditional social institutions in the context of the culture and civilisation in which one lives. Obviously, as Western society continually advances down an increasingly degenerate path where the destruction of traditional institutions and the dilution of Western culture are actively promoted, conservatism seems like a natural ally to the beleaguered Western man.

However nothing could be further from the truth. Conservatism is not an ideology of advancement or of progress – but merely one that is obsessed with clinging to and protecting the current status quo. Conservatism doesn't seek progress or to move society forward in a positive direction, but in fact simply seeks to retain what is currently in place. If one was to think of conservatism as a military strategy, it could be thought of as a strategy that was only concerned with occupying a line and defending that line against attack. To further this military analogy, conservatism is not concerned with advance, attack or counterattack – conservatism is simply concerned with the defence of a fixed position.

Due to the nature of conservatism as an almost purely defensive strategy, it is doomed to failure, just as any military force engaged in a war would be doomed if all it concerned itself with was an endless defence against an unending assault. At some point in any conflict, after successful defences have been secured, any force that seeks victory must in fact counterattack and attack again and again until its enemy is driven back and ultimately smashed and defeated.

Any military force that mounts a successful defence and then elects to simply sit back and wait for another attack on their position would be inviting their eventual defeat. For an army to sit back and wait for their enemy to attack and to allow that enemy to simply continue attacking is to allow that enemy the luxury of regrouping and improving their strategy. Over time that enemy will improve their strategy and will find weaknesses in the defenders' position and eventually – no matter how long it takes – will learn to exploit those weaknesses in order to achieve victory.

It may take weeks, months or even years – but as time passes the attacks on the defenders' position will become increasingly effective and strike with increasing fervour until eventually the defenders' position will weaken and crumble. The defenders are then faced with defeat which gives them no choice but to fall back and regroup and form a new line of defence, but this time the line of defence is set deeper within their own territory. Over time this process leads to a war of attrition, more and more lines of defence crumble and more and more territory is lost until eventually, those defending the current line can't even remember the position they once occupied let alone dream of reclaiming it!

This is exactly how the conservative operates in a political sense. The conservative only seeks to defend the current status quo and hold the current line or 'moral standpoint'; the conservative is only occupied with defending whatever his opponent chooses to attack and is not concerned with the larger political picture. The conservative sees the battle at hand and fights for the defence of what he or she sees as right and true, but does not see the larger picture of the war that surrounds that battle. As a consequence of the conservative's narrow view and defensive nature, in the long term the conservative is always doomed to fail.

The enemies of the West know the nature of conservatism and that is exactly why they approve so wholeheartedly of conservative parties and movements. In fact the enemies of the West make a concerted effort to direct into conservative movements those within Western society who have begun to wake up to the problems facing Western man. The enemies of the West are committed to victory, so ensuring those who seek to protect the West adopt a losing strategy is simply part of their long-term plan. For the enemies of the

West – as we have seen earlier – do not defend their position; they constantly attack and constantly push the envelope of the degeneracy ever further.

As the group that constantly attacks and is allowed to regroup and develop new strategies will constantly have the advantage over the group that simply chooses to defend a line, the enemies of the West know that their attacks will always eventually succeed and defeat the conservative. Eventually the conservative line will crumble and the enemies of the West will have made ever more ground in their unending assault on Western civilisation. Thus for the enemies of the West, it is always only a matter of time before their latest attack on Western man is successful.

Earlier it was discussed how the acceptable norms in film and music have changed over time and how those acceptable norms have slowly become ever more degenerate. What was once outrageous is now seen as passé and what is now outrageous would have been wholly unacceptable or even unthinkable just a few years ago. This method of pushing the envelope of what is acceptable, which over time causes the established norm to become ever more degenerate and debased, is not simply limited to what is displayed by the media.

The enemies of the West attack Western society through a variety of different channels – one of them is social policy. The conservative will adopt a position on social policy of upholding the current moral status quo and the enemies of the West will then proceed to attack that status quo with the aim of breaking down another set of moral values and furthering the push toward degeneracy and moral decay.

Over time, the conservative's position will face a relentless onslaught which will eventually force the conservative to concede on different points and give ground to his enemies, and social policy and acceptable moral norms will be constantly redrawn by those trying to destroy Western society and undermine its core values and social structures. This can be perfectly illustrated by examining social policy toward homosexuality in the United Kingdom and how in a few short years the political landscape surrounding that issue was forever changed.

Up until 1967 it was illegal to carry out homosexual acts in the UK, even in private. However, in 1967, the Sexual Offences Act decriminalised homosexual acts between two men over twenty-one years of age in private in England and Wales. This was a watershed moment – and something many conservative-minded folk were unhappy with. However, the assault on the conservative position on homosexuality did not stop at simply decriminalising sexual activity between two consenting adults over the age of twenty-one, this was just the beginning.

The conservative line that homosexuality should be illegal – even between two consenting adults – had been breached. Many would even say that the fall of this line was indeed reasonable, after all what two people do in their own homes as consenting adults (as long as they are not harming anyone) is their own business. But this was not the end of the matter, and those wishing to push the homosexual agenda on the West did not stop there.

Throughout the 1970s an increasing number of pro-homosexual groups sprang into existence and the first ever gay pride festival was held in London with over one thousand people in attendance. The original line held by conservatives that homosexuality should be illegal was now long forgotten, and despite homosexual acts being legalised between consenting adults in the privacy of their own homes, the push was now for public displays of homosexuality to become accepted and normalised. The conservatives who had given ground were now having their new position assaulted and increasingly that position was looking untenable.

This trend continued into the 1980s with an increased push for the normalisation and acceptance of those suffering from AIDS. Eventually the conservatives had to draw yet another line in the sand and erect another position to defend – this was Section 28. Section 28 was a law enacted in 1988 as an amendment to the United Kingdom's Local Government Act 1986, and stated that a local authority 'shall not intentionally promote homosexuality or publish material with the intention of promoting homosexuality', or 'promote the teaching in any maintained school of the acceptability of homosexuality as a pretended family relationship'.

The conservatives had made their new position clear and sought to erect a line that would never be breached. Whilst now they were happy with homosexuality being legal and were happy for ever increasing public displays of homosexuality, they would not stand for it being promoted as a normal or natural alternative to the heterosexual nuclear family. This new defensive line was drawn and the enemies of the West had a new target – and by 1994 the cracks were already showing in the conservatives' defences as the legal age of homosexual consent was dropped from twenty-one to eighteen.

In 2000 the assault on Section 28 intensified with legislation being drawn up to repeal the 1988 act. This was followed swiftly in 2001 by the lowering of the age of sexual consent for homosexual couples to sixteen – in line with that of heterosexual couples. The conservative line was now under heavy assault and cracks were showing everywhere – by 2002 it was enacted in law that homosexual couples could adopt children and the new homosexual family would be treated in the same way as the heterosexual family. In 2003 the line fell completely and Section 28 was scrapped; the conservative position had completely crumbled.

In 2004 Britain saw legalisation passed that legalised same sex civil partnerships, and by 2014 it was legal for homosexual couples to marry. By this time the conservatives were no longer even putting up a fight. It had taken just forty-seven years for homosexuality to go from being illegal in Britain to becoming on a complete par with heterosexuality, and to be promoted as a completely acceptable norm with homosexuals even granted the right to marry and adopt children, forming their own twisted version of the nuclear family.

This is of course just one example of how conservatives draw a line in the sand and defend a point only to see their line be pushed ever further backwards until they eventually see everything they once fought for smashed to pieces. What is worse is often the conservative position is forced back so far that conservatives can't even remember what they originally stood for in the first place. But the undeniable point that underlies all of this is that never once did the conservatives ever try to recapture the positions they had lost. Never once did the conservatives ever mount a counterattack or push forward to reclaim ground from their enemies.

The purely defensive strategy employed by conservatives is fatally flawed – conservatives accept defeat and are all too ready to accept the new position forced upon them by their enemies. The new position the conservative adopts is of course not their own position, but one that has been largely dictated to them by their enemies. This new position then becomes gospel and the old position is forgotten – an embarrassing relic of the past. Hence the sermon that the conservative preaches is not their own, but a bastardised set of policies largely influenced and twisted by the hand of their enemies.

By extension of this the conservative actually has disdain and disgust for fellow conservatives who talk of the old position – let alone those who would utter 'nonsense' about reclaiming that position. The conservative is now dancing to the tune of his enemies, so anyone who questions the new line or dares to suggest attempting to reclaim the old line is accused of not 'playing fair' and is henceforth excommunicated as an embarrassment or a heretic.

To return to the analogy of the military force, it is like the conservatives are conducting their military operations under the 'rules of engagement' set by their own enemies. The convention for political battle that sets the parameters, the acceptable language and the guidelines for political discourse is not overseen by conservatives – but by their enemies. However the conservatives rush to eagerly sign up to this convention on political battle in an effort to prove they are 'decent folk' and are 'playing fair'.

However there is no fair play; by signing up to rules of engagement that are dictated and drafted by your enemies you are effectively tying your own hands and limiting your own ability to fight. Conservatives always find themselves hampered because they have accepted rules that are designed to ensure that the conservative loses. The reason that conservatives do this is because they don't want to be seen by anyone as the 'bad guys' – they want to be seen to 'play fair'.

Conservatives adhere to these rules of 'fair play' not to impress their own supporters, but in a vain attempt to please the enemies of the West and those who support twisted anti-Western agendas. To seek to please those who wish to destroy you and defeat you in battle is a fatal flaw, and one that seals the fate of the conflict before it has even started. Essentially the way the conservative adheres to the rules laid out by his enemies could be likened to a boxer entering the ring with one hand tied behind his back.

This all serves to highlight another fatal flaw at the heart of conservatism – cowardice. The conservative is a craven coward who is desperate to be judged as a good person not just by his own supporters, but by those who are in fact his enemies. The conservative cares what others think of him regardless of whether they are friend or foe – and this fatal flaw leads to the conservative adopting the speech, the standards and the very moral code of those that he fights against in a vain effort to please those who seek to destroy everything he holds dear and everything he fights to protect.

If a member of a conservative group dares to challenge the enemy and to argue that a defensive line that has long fallen was in fact a noble and good position to hold, that individual will be pilloried. The problem lies in the fact that it is not just the conservatives' enemies that will attack the conservative that dares to speak out – but fellow conservatives will also shun the rogue conservative for daring to suggest that a previously held position could or should be reclaimed and is a position worth fighting for. After all, the conservative must be seen as playing fair and wouldn't like to be seen to offend anyone – even his enemies!

The enemies of the West do not play by the same rules though, and when one of their number attacks a conservative position in a way that would be deemed offensive, then excuses are made, the incident is swept under the carpet and life goes on. In fact it is often the case that when an individual comes forth with a particularly degenerate or offensive new attack upon Western morality, they go on to be labelled a 'visionary' or are simply regarded as being 'ahead of their time'.

Take for example the position of Section 28. Any conservative who now dared to sing the praises of this law (a law enacted by conservatives) would be literally flung out of any conservative organisation and labelled a 'homophobe', 'hater' and a 'bigot'. On the other hand, those pushing for increased 'sexual liberalisation' are often exposed for having links with paedophile rings, yet no one is sacked or demoted and enquiries are never commissioned.

The craven cowardice of the conservative, and the way that the conservative position has crumbled, can be seen by the fact that the same Conservative Party who formed the government in 1988 and passed Section 28 as law went on to be the government that passed the law to legalise gay marriage in 2014.

Of course, the conservative would laugh all this off and simply state that the conservative mind is 'progressive'. But exactly whose definition of 'progress' does this adhere to? Every single 'progression' that the conservative has made has been in the direction that the enemy of the conservative has pushed for. Not once has the conservative ever made progress in any other direction – fundamentally because conservatives never seek to recover the ground they have lost or discuss policy that may offend their enemies, as the conservative is playing by a set of rules designed to ensure his defeat.

The fact that the word 'progressive' is an adjective that conservatives would happily use to describe themselves shows just how far conservatives will go to please their enemies. There is nothing 'progressive' about giving ground to one's enemies – and no progress can ever be made when one is committed to using the language and terminology created by those enemies.

The conservative could be seen like cliffs that line a beach. They stand strong and tall and look immovable, but over a period of time they are reduced to nothing and washed away by the tide. The cliffs never make progress, they never rebuild, they are simply eroded by the sea. Eventually the cliffs are just a memory and everything that they once were is gone.

If one were to take a look at the current manifesto of the leading conservative party in any Western nation, that manifesto would bear no resemblance to the same party's manifesto fifty years ago. In fact, if one were to read those two manifestos, they would illustrate a pattern of defeat and withdrawal and the weakening of the party's core policies.

To win a war, one cannot simply focus on a single battle or a single line of defence. To win a war one must look at the big picture and analyse the wider situation at hand. To achieve victory one cannot simply be obsessed with defence, but one must be willing to advance and to gain ground and eventually be willing to do what is necessary to drive one's enemy into the sea. The enemies of the West know this – and they adopt this strategy of continually pushing forward in order to further their objectives.

Hence to defeat the enemies of the West, Western man must adopt a mindset that at its core has a strong ideology and set of values that do not shift and bend to pander to the opinions and sensibilities of those who wish to destroy the West. To defeat the enemies of the West, Western man must be as tenacious and committed as his foes, and must not just defend his position, but also must seek to gain ground and fight to push forward his own ideals and beliefs.

If Western man is to defeat the enemies of the West, he will not do so by tailoring his arguments and formulating his strategies in order to please those who seek to destroy him. Western man cannot play by the rules of his enemies and then hope to defeat those enemies. The rules that conservatives adhere to are designed in such a way to ensure that the conservative can't possibly win.

Conservatism is not a solution for the problems of the West. Conservatism is the creeping death of the West. Conservatism is simply a false alternative to the madness and degeneracy pushed by the enemies of the West and one that has been set up to be knocked down. If the enemies of the West seek to push madness upon the Western world as quickly as possible, conservatism is simply a force that slows that madness. If the enemies of the West are driving Western man over the edge of a cliff to his annihilation, conservatives simply ensure that process takes a little longer – Western man still ends up going over the edge of the cliff, but it just takes him longer to get there!

Western man needs a real alternative, a real force that can and will fight back against the enemies of the West and one that will not cower and creep in order to play the 'nice guy'.

22
FALSE SALVATION – LIBERTARIANISM

Western society was once a perfect society and the underlying force that creates a 'perfect society' is the cohesiveness of the people that make up that society. A group of people must have a strong set of shared morals and values in order to function as a community. These shared morals and values are what enable a group of people to develop a community consciousness. The community consciousness within Western society has been termed the Western superego. Once a group of people has developed a community consciousness, the individuals that make up that community can work together in harmony and are able to achieve more as a group than they ever could have achieved alone.

The enemies of the West seek to undermine the cohesive nature of Western society and have done so in many devious ways that have already been discussed at length. The final push of the attack on the West is one that seeks to ensure a cohesive society no longer exists, and that Western man pursues individualism rather than the goal of a homogenous community. A group of disparate individuals all focusing on their own needs do not function as a community. As such, a disparate group of individuals would be far easier to conquer than a cohesive community which is able to pull together for the greater good.

Bearing this in mind, it is curious that some of those who are supposedly committed to traditionalism and the defence of Western culture have adopted libertarianism as a way in which to seek to defend traditionalism and Western culture. Libertarianism has been seen by some as the perfect defence against the enemies of the West and a way to ideologically undermine the attacks that are aimed at Western civilisation.

Libertarianism (Latin: *liber,* 'free') is a political philosophy that upholds liberty as its principal objective. Libertarians seek to maximize autonomy and freedom of choice, emphasizing political freedom, voluntary association and the primacy of individual judgment. Ultimately, Libertarianism can be boiled down to the following short principle: everyone has the right to do as they wish as long as they don't infringe on the rights of others.

Libertarianism can clearly be seen as individualistic and favours the rights of the individual above the notion of a community or a state. But therein lays the problem – if individualism and the destruction of a cohesive community is the bane of the West, the West's salvation surely cannot be found in the embrace of a political ideology that at its heart values individualism above the good of the community.

The draw of libertarianism is simple – it sounds like the most perfect and fair standpoint that one can take, and thus appears on the surface very difficult to argue with. After all, what is more fair and just than allowing each person to follow their own will and maintaining a state where everyone tolerates one another despite their different political, cultural or religious affiliations? But 'tolerance' is one of the dubious virtues that got Western man into the dire situation he faces today. In fact, Aristotle said it best: 'Tolerance and apathy are the last virtues of a dying society'.

It is Western man's tolerance of the degeneracy that is pushed upon him that has undermined Western culture and has led to the decline of the West. The same tolerance that has damaged the West is at the heart of libertarianism, a tolerance that meekly states that we should all have the right to live our lives the way we see fit. But is it not right to be intolerant of things that appal you? Is it not right to be intolerant of the things that threaten your loved ones, your family and your community? Is it not right to be intolerant of the things that ultimately threaten your very way of life and that threaten Western civilisation itself?

Tolerance isn't a virtue and it certainly isn't something that Western man should embrace. Tolerance is a key part of the mindset that has allowed the enemies of the West to get as far as they have. In fact tolerance is one of the favoured buzz words used by the enemies of the West and is often deployed to silence criticism of anti-Western social policy and the degeneracy that has engulfed Western civilisation. Libertarians also like to make use of the word tolerance. In doing so they smugly believe they are using a form of 'mental judo' whereby they make use of the words and phrases created by the enemies of the West for their own ends. This mental judo is an attempt to ensnare the enemies of the West in their own traps and tie them up with their own logic.

After all – if traditionalists and conservatives must be tolerant of every degenerate fad and subculture, surely those who partake in those degenerate fads and subcultures must repay the favour and be tolerant of the traditionalists and conservatives? This almost sounds good, and to the less discerning reader it may sound like a viable plan of defence against the enemies of the West. What could be cleverer than to use the structures and 'game rules' created by the enemies of the West in order to win the game? To turn those rules against the very people who created them, essentially forcing the enemies of the West onto their own swords, would surely be a sound plan.

Sadly, to believe that the battle for the Western mind can be won by playing within the rules laid out by those who wish to destroy Western civilisation is at best wishful thinking and at worst utterly naïve. By agreeing to tolerate degeneracy – on the condition that those who follow that degeneracy in turn tolerate decency – is a recipe for disaster. By tolerating degeneracy and agreeing to live in a society where that degeneracy is prevalent, you are agreeing to immerse yourself in the filth rather than aiming to create something better.

Imagine owning a sharp new suit. You want to wear your suit and obviously you want to keep the suit clean and in good condition. Now imagine you are forced to wear it in a sewer. It would not matter how hard you tried, how much painstaking effort you went to in order to preserve the suit – if you were surrounded by filth and grime, eventually the suit would be covered in filth and grime too. The point is, if you're living in the sewer – eventually you're going to get covered in faeces – not the most pleasant of analogies, but one that perfectly fits the ideology of libertarianism.

Take this analogy and extrapolate it to a real world scenario. You live on a street with your wife and children. You are a traditionalist; you believe in God, your own Western culture, the nuclear family and you believe that traditional Western morality is what any healthy society should embrace. However your neighbours to one side are a homosexual couple with an adopted Somalian child, and they believe in throwing large parties for their promiscuous group of friends. Your neighbours to the other side believe in recreational drug use, hedonism and have an open relationship and indulge in regular sex parties. Your neighbour across the street is a single mother with seven different children to six different men; her children are never disciplined, her house lies in ruin and her children regularly wander around in a dirty and dishevelled state.

But under libertarianism, all of that is fine and should be tolerated. As long as your neighbours all respect your right to live as you wish and raise your children the way you want, you should respect their right to do the same. But does that really sound like a healthy and pleasant way to live and raise a family? Would an upstanding Western family really want to be surrounded by the kind of degeneracy depicted earlier? Of course not! To bring one's family up around those kind of influences, despite whether they were openly hostile toward your family or not, would be suicidal.

To tolerate your family living in that situation would not make you a good or strong person; it would make you negligent. It would be no different to the man living in the sewer wearing his new suit – eventually the filth would end up corrupting what was once pristine and perfect. The influences that surround you go on to affect and shape you – this is especially true for young people. As we have discussed at length, this is exactly why the enemies of the West seek to target the young with such subversive and damaging material.

But mutual tolerance and acceptance is the cornerstone of a libertarian society, so anything good and wholesome can be surrounded by anything that is degenerate and twisted – as long as both agree to accept and respect each other. The effect of this is clear: the wholesome family would slowly be subverted and twisted as that family would be surrounded and influenced by everything that is rotten and harmful.

Aristotle did not only attack the dubious virtue of tolerance, but he also attacked apathy. Apathy however seems to be the other key 'virtue' of the libertarian ideology. For an individual to allow the sickness on his doorstep to go unchallenged would be very revealing. To be surrounded by degeneracy and to not want to do anything about that degeneracy is negligent. But libertarianism is more concerned with self than with community, so as long as everyone agrees to respect each other's choices, the libertarian must allow those who have been led down the wrong path to continue indulging in damaging behaviour. This is the opposite of what should occur in any healthy community. When a conscientious individual sees something wrong within their community, they should not only refuse to tolerate that wrong, but also seek to fix it.

The key to Western society is community – and libertarianism isn't about community; it is an abstract political ideology concerned with promoting the good of the individual in a desperate attempt to ideologically outdo those who wish to destroy Western man. If you were to reverse the nightmarish situation in the neighbourhood described earlier and instead your neighbours were all functioning nuclear families, one father was the local pastor, one mother was the local Girl Guide leader, another father was the local tennis coach and so on – surely that would be a better situation in which to live and bring up a family – a homogenous society where everyone is an upstanding individual.

Your children would not only have a healthy home life where strong role models imparted moral values and traditions to them – but the same would also be true outside of the home. Wherever your children went on your street they would see similar nuclear families, strong parents, well-behaved children, clean homes and strong adult role models. That kind of society is what made Western civilisation strong and what helped generation after generation of young people develop their superego.

That is of course what Western man should be aiming for – a return to the strong homogenous values and community bonds that built Western civilisation. Libertarianism doesn't strive for that; instead it is a weak cry of 'if I leave you alone and tolerate you, will you leave me alone and tolerate me?' It is like the cry of a beaten and defeated man who can take no more and simply begs for some form of truce or stalemate in order to hold onto the last scraps of what he once fought for. This cry is not the cry of the warrior, and it is not the cry of the man who seeks to win the war and drive out his enemies. It is the cry of the man who simply wishes to be left alone hoping that whilst Rome burns his house doesn't catch fire.

Whilst conservatives stand together and hold a line, nervously moderating their speech and political message in a vain attempt to appeal to their enemies, libertarians have a different but equally suicidal tactic. The libertarians cry that as long as they are left alone as individuals to pursue whatever they wish, the enemies of the West can do as they wish and live as they want and promote what they see fit. Both ideologies lead to only one eventuality – defeat for Western man.

Inevitably the conservatives' moral line collapses and they are pushed back, slowly over time becoming everything they once stood against. Whilst the libertarian does not see his position collapse, he does face an equally grim fate. Over time the libertarian stands as an increasingly isolated voice of sanity in a sea of madness, simply watching as everything he loves is engulfed by everything he hates, forlornly trying to stand against the tide whilst equally claiming to tolerate the very tide that seeks to sweep him away.

Libertarianism is another ideology that is tolerated by the enemies of the West. Libertarianism is not smiled upon in the same way as conservatism, as libertarianism does throw up more problems for those who seek to destroy Western civilisation. But nevertheless, the enemies of the West know that libertarianism is not a winning strategy for Western man.

Earlier, the conservative was likened to the cliffs that line a beach. The cliffs stand strong and tall and look immovable, but over a period of time they are reduced to nothing and washed away by the tide. The cliffs never make progress, they never rebuild, they are simply eroded by the sea until they are merely sand on the beach. Eventually the once mighty and imposing cliffs are just a memory and everything that they once were is gone.

If the conservative was seen as the cliffs, the libertarian can be viewed as the rocky outcrop that stands strong even after the sea has washed away the other rocks and pushed the line of the cliffs further back inland. The libertarian is the proud shard of stronger rock that still stands tall even though it is surrounded by the sea. However, that shard of rock is isolated and completely cut off from the mainland, ultimately standing without purpose as the sea keeps on advancing regardless of its stand. Eventually the outcrop falls; it might have stood longer than the rest of the line of cliffs, but it has not halted the advance of the tide.

Of course that is the key reason why the enemies of the West tolerate libertarianism – they know that one or two dissenting voices who pledge to 'tolerate' the degeneracy are simply like outcrops of rock that stand in the sea – isolated and ineffective. The enemies of the West understand that the key to Western society is Western man's community consciousness. The key to Western society is a sense of underlying homogenous moral values and traditions that build the Western superego. Libertarianism focuses on the individual, the very opposite of what Western man needs to focus on.

The libertarian will argue that retaining one's own individuality and strength is the key to defeating the enemies of the West. The libertarian will claim that over time when the weaker individuals in society slowly descend into madness, and their lifestyle ultimately leads to their own demise, the strong and moral individuals will be all that will remain as a shining beacon of hope that will lead to the rebirth of the West. This is of course wishful thinking – and crucially would only apply in a society that was made up of one homogenous group that had simply fractured over time.

However, Western man does not live in a homogenous perfect society, and due to mass immigration Western man is now surrounded in his own homeland by numerous different cultures and religions which have not succumbed to the same drive for individuality as Western man has. These other cultures that have retained their homogeneity will eventually grow and engulf more and more of the Western world. Foreign cultures that have emigrated to the West have retained their strength and community spirit, at the same time Western man has embraced individualism and is being out-bred, leaving no chance of a miraculous rebirth. So no matter how strong the libertarian's stand is against degeneracy, as an isolated individual he can never fight back against demographics – only a large and cohesive community can mount that fightback.

The libertarian may have an ideological position that enables him to win a few moral debates against the enemies of the West; however libertarianism still leaves Western man in a poor predicament. When Western man faces other cultures that have settled in his homeland, he does so as a disparate group of individuals. Despite the libertarian managing to stay true to his beliefs and hold on as a moral beacon in a sea of filth, that one lone beacon cannot stand against a strong and united community. Only if Western man stands as a cohesive community can he stand against the potential threat of a foreign community within his own borders that seeks aggressive expansion and growth.

Never forget, the reason Western civilisation scaled such magnificent heights is because the individuals who made up Western society worked as one, which allowed them to achieve more than they could from simply working alone. Western society was truly more than the sum of its parts. Individuals may develop great inventions – but it is a cohesive society that puts those great inventions into production. That same society can then put those inventions to use on a grand scale, allowing those inventions to make a difference that can shape the world.

The libertarian stands alone or in a small and isolated group. Regardless of what the libertarian creates or invents, he doesn't have the will of a great society to ensure his creations reach their maximum potential. What's more, the libertarian also lacks the strong and powerful community needed to protect his creations. Libertarians do not build great cities or raise great armies to protect those cities. Should the individuals who make up Western society embrace libertarianism – who does the onus then fall upon when it comes to protecting Western society?

Does the libertarian cravenly fall to his knees in front of an invading force and beg 'leave me and my family alone and we shall tolerate you and your new laws and ways'? How does this compare with the men of the West who showed their Western heart by standing against overwhelming numbers in order to protect the community from which they came? But crucially, the individual cannot stand against a cohesive invading force – and this is a fact the enemies of the West know all too well.

Ultimately, just like conservatism, libertarianism is simply the slow and creeping death of the West. It does not offer a solution to the death of the Western superego – nor does it offer a solution to the endless torrent of attacks perpetuated by the enemies of the West. Libertarianism simply offers a weak cry for those who wish to be left alone, in hope that in being left alone they may live out their days in the way they see fit. Libertarianism does not care for the very community that built Western civilisation; it is a selfish ideology that centres on the individual and his or her own personal will to survive.

The libertarian simply ensures the survival of himself and his immediate family without thinking of the greater good of the community. If the libertarian does ensure his own survival, what shall be his prize and his legacy? Quite simply he will survive to bear witness to the last days of the West. The libertarian can stand and watch as Western civilisation crumbles, knowing that he is the last of his kind – that is his reward for his selfish nature. The libertarian will have to live with the fact that he tolerated all that was evil in order to secure an easy life for himself and his immediate family.

Tolerance and apathy are not virtues; tolerance and apathy are exactly what the enemies of the West wish for Western man to embrace. Tolerance is the ability or willingness to tolerate the existence of opinions or behaviour that one dislikes or disagrees with. Apathy is a lack of interest, enthusiasm or concern. These two 'virtues' are the mental sicknesses that have allowed Western man to sit in silence and do nothing as the vile degeneracy pushed by the enemies of the West has become ever more commonplace within Western society. To tolerate those that wish to destroy you, and to do nothing about the damage they inflict upon you, is not a virtue but a sin against yourself and your people.

To defeat the enemies of the West, Western man must rise again as a community and not only refuse to tolerate the sickness pushed upon him, but actively strive to combat that sickness and fight for a brighter and healthier future.

23

FALSE SALVATION – THE HOLLYWOOD NAZI

National Socialism is an ideology of discipline and order that seeks to establish a perfect homogenous society that is centred on national unity. As such National Socialism scorns social divisions and selfish individualism. National Socialism is an ideology that strives for excellence and pushes individuals within society to better themselves – not just for the sake of individual greatness but instead to improve society as a whole.

Discipline, order and excellence made National Socialism one of the few true threats to the enemies of the West – so what better way to undermine National Socialism than to take its symbols and banners and wrap them around a degenerate musical subculture? The enemies of the West fear the power of National Socialism, and know that in its true and pure form it is a uniting force that could drive the enemies of the West from Western shores and free Western man.

The enemies of the West have sought to attack National Socialism and undermine it. The enemies of the West have used their power in the media and the press to 'rebrand' National Socialism in the most degenerate and debased way possible. The enemies of the West have sought to turn National Socialism on its head and ensure that instead of discipline, order and excellence, National Socialism stands for the opposite of these things – chaos, degeneracy and weakness.

The enemies of the West have created what is known as the 'Hollywood Nazi', otherwise known as the skinhead. The Hollywood Nazi is anything but a National Socialist. The Hollywood Nazi may well emblazon National Socialist symbols on his clothes; he may well stand in front of banners that bear those symbols, and he may also espouse his wish to save Western man, but the Hollywood Nazi is a twisted vision of genuine National Socialism. Hollywood Nazism and the skinhead music scene that accompanies it have become a beacon for defectives and misfits who are attracted to being part of an 'outsider gang' that has a reputation for being anti-social.

The Hollywood Nazi was created by the same twisted minds that gave the Western world Lady Gaga and *Rebel Without a Cause*. The enemies of the West created the Hollywood Nazi subculture and propagated their creation through the media by producing films such as *Romper Stomper* and *American History X*. These films attempt to redefine National Socialism along lines that are beneficial to the enemies of the West. These films also attempt to associate racial and cultural consciousness with negatives that are intended to drive normal people away from having anything to do with any form of nationalism.

The films that promote the Hollywood Nazi are made by the enemies of the West in order to appeal to lost and self-destructive youngsters. These films seek to push negative role models and a destructive subculture upon young Western minds in a similar manner to films like *Kids* and *Rebel Without a Cause*. What makes the Hollywood Nazi subculture unique is that it has a second objective – it seeks to present nationalism as both unappealing and toxic. The Hollywood Nazi subculture is unique as it is used to scare the public away from nationalism.

Young people who choose to rebel against their parents and society by adopting the skinhead subculture strive to conform to the image of the Hollywood Nazi. This begins a self-fulfilling cycle which serves the aims of the enemies of the West. Young people see films like *Romper Stomper,* and then seek to emulate the characters in those films. Then the media film real life documentaries based on violent skinhead gangs who attempt to replicate the behaviour, dress and attitudes of characters they saw in films. These gangs are filmed drinking, being anti-social, engaging in acts of violence and attacking immigrants all in the name of nationalism. This is the way the enemies of the West have turned their twisted fantasy of nationalism into a damaging reality.

The first important thing to discuss when analysing this false salvation is to compare the Hollywood Nazi with genuine National Socialism. To do this let us first take a look at one of the defining moments in National Socialist history – the Nuremberg Rallies. The Nuremberg Rallies were the annual party rallies held by the NSDAP (Nationalsozialistische Deutsche Arbeiterpartei – National Socialist German Workers' Party) between 1923 and 1938. Arguably the most famous of these rallies occurred in 1934 and was the subject of the film the *Triumph of the Will,* directed and produced by Leni Riefenstahl. In 1934 over 700,000 National Socialists attended the Nuremburg rally – a true spectacle for the world to behold.

The Nuremberg Rallies centred on political speeches and large orderly parades – discipline and order were central to the entire event, and the musical accompaniment was classical orchestral overtures. The sight of hundreds of thousands of men lined up in perfect order, listening to speeches made under huge banners, was a sight to behold, and something that one would have been proud to be a part of. Those in attendance wore uniforms, looked healthy and were of good breeding stock. Everyone in attendance looked alike and were clearly part of one cohesive group.

Compare the Nuremberg Rallies with the kind of events held by modern Hollywood Nazis or skinheads. Skinhead events consist of a few hundred people gathered in a small hall, drinking, smoking, pushing one another and listening to raucous music. In fact the modern skinhead event couldn't be much further from the Nuremburg Rallies in either intent or execution. The whole ethos behind these skinhead events has nothing whatsoever to do with order or discipline and in fact is centred on chaos. There are no orderly speeches, parades or shows of strength and those in attendance are neither uniformed nor smart in their appearance.

Obese men covered with tattoos lurch back and forth in a drunken manner as they listen to music which clearly has more in common with the degenerate subcultures pushed by the enemies of the West than it does with anything healthy or classical. There is no culture and no spectacle – in fact if one changed the lyrics of the music and removed the banners at the back of the stage these events could belong to any musical subculture. In fact without the lyrics and banners those in attendance could be mistaken for punks, goths or rockers and seen as just another group of misled individuals attached to a subculture manufactured by the enemies of the West.

These skinhead events are based on exactly the same kind of hedonism, degeneracy and individualism as other musical events and subcultures created by the enemies of the West. These events are not spectacles of excellence attended by fit, healthy and clean-living men that would hold the world in awe. These events are spectacles of degeneracy which would actually appal most normal people and dissuade them from joining any form of nationalist movement.

Whereas the Nuremburg Rallies and the film *Triumph of the Will* united a nation behind a common cause and showed the world what could be achieved by a homogenous, organised and disciplined organisation, skinhead concerts do the opposite. If taken to their logical extreme these skinhead events would be no different to the hedonistic festivals where young people drink excessively, use drugs and behave wildly for a weekend – a far cry from what Western man should be aiming for.

If one looks back to what was put forward as a perfect society, an analogy was drawn with a colony of bees. This analogy illustrated order, discipline and an entire community moving in unison toward one goal. The Nuremburg Rallies were the human embodiment of that perfect society and a showcase of that order – hundreds of thousands of men in uniform who looked the same, moving in unison and order as a display of power and discipline. Compare that with a skinhead concert, where drunken individuals wearing customised clothing and exhibiting outlandish body modifications and tattoos move in a chaotic fashion as they jump around aimlessly. These two events are literally polar opposites – yet the enemies of the West have tried to link them and pass them off as one and the same!

This analysis will surely cause raised eyebrows – after all those attending these events allegedly subscribe to the higher ideals of nationalism and would happily describe themselves as National Socialists. However actions speak louder than words. To be a

National Socialist is not merely to raise a flag or pay lip service to certain facets of an ideology. To be a National Socialist is to live a clean and healthy lifestyle and aim to be the best you can be – physically, mentally and spiritually. To be a National Socialist is to be ordered, disciplined and strong and uphold the values and traditions of the West.

Most importantly, National Socialism promotes the notion that one should strive to be the best one can be; it promotes self-improvement and the pursuit of a healthy ideal self. To follow the skinhead way is to do the very opposite of this and to embrace the very things the enemies of the West have used in order to destroy Western man and break apart Western communities.

By creating a degenerate musical subculture and attaching it to National Socialism (thus creating the Hollywood Nazi), the enemies of the West have made this corrupted version of National Socialism a magnet for defectives. Often those who are attracted to the skinhead scene are lost individuals who cannot function in society and are seeking to be part of a group of other anti-social misfits. These people are not captains of industry, great athletes, inventors or other inspirational individuals, but often the opposite.

The Hollywood Nazi subculture is designed to scoop up these defectives. Take the film *Romper Stomper:* the skinheads in that film live like animals in an abandoned warehouse. They are essentially squatters who do not work, do not pay rent, and do not provide anything productive to society. Minus the flags, banners and patches they would be seen as common or garden delinquents and undesirables. What kind of person would be drawn to that lifestyle – certainly not the people required to mount a serious fightback in order to save the West.

Not only do the people who flock to this scene provide little or no benefit to the wider nationalist cause, they are in fact poisonous to the greater good and inhibit the growth of nationalism. These defectives alienate nationalism from the very people it needs to attract if it is ever to grow and become a genuine alternative. Why would a man who owns a successful business wish to join a group of homeless bums who squat in a warehouse and drink until 4am every morning? Why would a loving mother and good housekeeper want to associate herself with a gang whose idea of political activity is spray-painting obscenities on toilet walls?

The healthy and normal people that nationalism needs to attract in order to grow and prosper want nothing to do with anti-social yobs or gangs. By wrapping up National Socialism in such negatives, the enemies of the West have actually pulled a very clever trick – they have ensured that normal and productive people will never again be drawn towards a genuine alternative to their poison.

Take for example a Western family who feel threatened by the loss of their culture, by the growing level of non-Western immigration into their town and who dislike the degeneracy that is pushed upon their children. When they look at alternatives to the current political system they want something that is a genuine alternative – something that presents a viable solution to the problems they face. The people who see gang culture as a growing problem within their towns and cities are hardly going to join a gang themselves. In fact they want the opposite of a gang: they want a strong and healthy community-based group that embodies the values they hold dear.

Therein lies the core of the problem – the Hollywood Nazi has more in common with black inner city gangs than he would like to admit. The big differences between black gangs and skinhead gangs are simply skin colour and musical taste. If upstanding families are unlikely to embrace black gang culture, then why would they embrace white gang culture? In fact most normal healthy-minded people would be opposed to violent anti-social gangs whatever the colour of their members or their supposed motivations. Healthy-minded people are not going to be driving around with black gangs throwing up gang signs and listening to obnoxious rap music, nor will they be sewing patches onto bomber jackets, listening to skinhead music and spray-painting racial slurs on the subway.

In fact it would be reasonable to state that a normal working family with healthy moral values and a healthy interest in traditionalism would have more in common with a family from another culture or ethnicity that worked hard, looked after their children and led a clean-living life than they would with a gang of skinheads. The Hollywood Nazi then becomes a self-reinforcing problem – the more social outcasts that become attracted to the 'scene', the more normal people are put off joining a nationalist alternative. This makes nationalism unattractive and forces normal people into the arms of other false salvations like conservatism and libertarianism.

The skinhead movement is wrapped up with violence and often the themes of racial violence are part of the music and general culture (if you can attribute a word such as 'culture' to this movement). Skinheads have become synonymous with racial attacks and the abuse of other racial groups. By perpetuating a violent stereotype, the skinhead is portrayed as a bully and someone who picks on easy targets. This is neither brave nor something that decent people would applaud. For every attack on a corner shop or lone member of an ethnic minority, those perpetrating such attacks drive countless thousands of normal people away from nationalism.

For normal family orientated folk, the idea of attacking a home or a business is abhorrent, and most decent people will naturally empathise with and have sympathy for those who face such abuse. Normal people would imagine how they would feel if their shop or home had just had its windows broken and would feel sympathy for the victim. This kind of sympathy leads regular people to turn their backs on nationalism. Normal law-abiding folk who have suffered at the hands of aggressive foreign cultures do not wish to victimise or attack innocent people as a response. Normal people who have suffered at the hands of aggressive foreign cultures wish for a disciplined and ordered response that is both lawful and fair. Only order and discipline can defeat chaos and madness.

Genuine National Socialism is not based on negativity or 'race hate'. Genuine National Socialism is based on love, a love for one's own people, a love for one's own land and a love for one's culture and traditions. The enemies of the West know that wrapping up a movement or organisation with race hate, especially with the accusation of 'racist' being so powerful, is a death blow to any chance of real growth or success. Racism, hatred and the belief in an all-encompassing racial conflict are often central tenets of the skinhead movement, something that makes that movement even more toxic to normal people.

But therein lies the other massive problem at the heart of Hollywood Nazism – the central belief that there will one day be a racial or religious conflict that will engulf society. The skinhead subculture largely subscribes to the misguided notion that one day, when such a conflict occurs, Western man will be forced to choose a side and will ultimately stand and fight with the skinheads in order to preserve the future of the West. As extensively discussed earlier, it is highly unlikely there will be such a conflict – and even if there was, Western man would not fare favourably.

Those attracted to the skinhead scene are often escapists and fantasists; they choose to live out their fantasies by attaching themselves to nationalism. They wish to believe in a fantasy where society collapses and a great conflict takes place that sees them emerge as the victors and as such the saviours of Western civilisation. This could not be further from the truth – and even if it was true, what would society be like once the skinheads had won this glorious war? How would the obese, warehouse dwelling, welfare claiming gang members rebuild the West after their glorious victory?

In reality though, most of the people who choose to believe in this scenario and attach themselves to this degenerate subculture are not fit enough, well-disciplined enough or well-trained enough to win a war. What's more, if faced with the choice of joining a skinhead gang or going it alone and risking the wrath of immigrant gangs, most normal Western families would be torn between the two and probably just curl up in their homes awaiting the outcome of the battle and quietly accepting their fate regardless.

As stated earlier, people group together based on shared values and feel more comfortable around those they identify closely with. Just as other subcultures and groups prevent Western man from coming together as one cohesive body, skinheads serve to add to this problem. In the event of a great collapse or 'race war' skinheads would not be a uniting force for Western man. Skinheads are just another musical subculture, and as such they further add to the fragmentation that plagues Western society.

When it comes to the idea of a civil war ripping apart a nation, and in this case a civil war that would involve different ethnic groups fighting one another, the key to victory would be readiness. The odd thing about skinheads – and what leads any educated observer to believe they are simply escapists – is that they are not prepared. Any group that seriously believed a great war was imminent would prioritise preparation and training above all other activities. Physical fitness, martial arts and survival skills would all rank highly on the checklist of those preparing themselves for a civil war and the inevitability of fighting in the streets.

Yet those who are constantly talking about fighting the enemy in the street are not making adequate preparations for such an occurrence. Talk of such violence is simply something these people get a buzz from; they get a kick from believing they are part of a resistance group that will one day be victorious in battle. In the same way that people who play fantasy role-playing games dream of assaulting castles full of orcs and goblins, the Hollywood Nazi dreams of storming through the streets and waging a guerrilla war. But just like orcs and goblins, this race war is a fantasy.

The 'skinhead way of life' is a far cry from the way of life that would be conducive to preparing for a civil war. In fact, anyone seriously preparing for armed conflict wouldn't be piling on the pounds, drinking copious amounts of cheap lager and spending what money they had left on tattoos. Health and fitness should be central to a National Socialist's life, and even more so if one believes that armed conflict is almost upon the West. Instead, the skinhead appears to be looking for some form of politically incorrect diversion. The individual drawn to the skinhead gang seeks to satiate the same drive for attention and self-gratification that drives others to join equally pointless groups such as punks or goths.

The Hollywood Nazi may wrap himself up in the banners of National Socialism and profess a love for Western man, but in reality the Hollywood Nazi or skinhead could not be further from what real National Socialism espouses. Order, discipline, uniforms, marches, fitness and positivity were all central to National Socialism and are the polar opposites of the behaviour that the Hollywood Nazi engages in. Drunken, obese, heavily tattooed and degenerate; the Hollywood Nazi would never have been welcomed into National Socialist organisations in the 1930s. In fact it would be fair to say that many of those who follow the path of the Hollywood Nazi would have been seen as undesirables and would have been interned in work camps had they lived under the rule of the NSDAP.

Can you imagine the faces of the massed ranks at the Nuremburg Rallies if they were to see the goings-on at a skinhead concert? Do you think they would be proud that the banners they served under were now the backdrop to a drunken party? The truth is, had the National Socialist party in Germany subscribed to the doctrine of the Hollywood Nazi it would never have come to power – and that is exactly the reason why the enemies of the West have created such a subculture.

The Hollywood Nazi wasn't invented to ensure Western man rediscovered the right path in life and freed his folk from the clutches of his enemies. The Hollywood Nazi was invented as a false salvation and to ensure normal people would never again turn to nationalism – the greatest threat the enemies of the West have ever faced.

For nationalism to win, it needs to attract winners – not losers. If nationalists continue to embrace the false salvation of Hollywood Nazism, they will ensure that nationalism will always end up on the losing side. Once any cause becomes a beacon for the losers within society, that cause is destined to fail.

24
TRUE SALVATION – NATIONALISM

The only true salvation for Western man is nationalism. Western man must return to his roots and embrace what once made him great. Western man must take on an ideology that encourages him to reconnect with his brothers and sisters and that allows him to rebuild his shattered communities. This ideology must reconnect Western man not only with his kin – but must also reconnect him with the land and soil that has been his home for thousands of years. Blood and soil are the natural callings that must be at the centre of Western man's mindset.

But Western man must do more than simply strive to reconnect with blood and soil – Western man must also strive for excellence. This drive for excellence must start with the individual, but it must not be for individual glory, instead this drive for excellence must be for a greater good. Western man must strive for excellence in order to become a beacon of hope around which others can cluster, a beacon that attracts others who wish to embrace a healthier way of life. In this way, Western man can begin to rebuild his fractured communities and create something better.

Western man must improve himself and hold his hand out to his brothers and sisters and aim to improve their lives also. Western man must work to tear down the barriers that have been erected in order to separate him from his kin and break up his once cohesive communities. Western man must rise up and embrace the single ideology that embodies all these virtues – nationalism. Western man must stand against both capitalism and communism and overcome social divisions to create a homogeneous society, and at the heart of this society must be tradition, culture and heritage.

The first and central tenet of nationalism is love for one's own race – genuine nationalism is not an ideology of hate for others, but a love for and devotion to one's own people and culture.

**To love one's own people and to respect all others
who wish to do the same.**

Nationalism wishes for Western man to embrace his own blood and rebuild the Western community. To be at peace with the world, a man must love himself and his own family and community – to hate your own people and to be riddled with false guilt will never lead to happiness or fulfilment. Nationalism is an ideology that elevates one's own people above all others and places the protection and love of those people above all other concerns.

Hatred for other people or races who also wish to follow a path of nationalism is wholly counterproductive. If Africans, Asians or any other ethnicity for that matter wish to embrace their own people and culture and strive for self-determination, then they should be applauded for doing so. The world is a magnificent place and is made up of an intricate tapestry of different cultures, races and ethnicities – and should remain that way.

Every race and culture should have the right to self-determination and self-governance.

No race or ethnicity should seek to dominate another: let the African be an African, let the Asian be an Asian – but equally let Western man be what he should be. Every race or culture should have the right to determine their own future and the direction their people take without interference or coercion from another. The world is a richer place for the existence of different cultures and ways of life – and it should remain so. Different people should not be forced to live together in one big melting pot which will inevitably lead to conflict and the loss of unique ways of life that have been evolving and developing for thousands of years.

Whilst different races and cultures cannot live in one confined space, there is enough room on this planet for everyone and everyone should have their own place.

All peoples of the world have the right to a homeland and the right to defend that homeland.

Western man has the right to the lands that gave birth to him, the lands that he has tended for thousands of years and the lands that have sheltered generations of his family – those lands are his birthright. Equally, all races of the world have the right to their own homelands too, and they have the right to live in those homelands in peace, free of interference from others. Every race has the right to defend their homeland against an aggressor that seeks to displace them or dominate them by either force or guile.

As such, every race and every nation has the right to control its own borders and limit immigration as they see fit. No nation is under any obligation to allow other cultures, races or ethnicities to cross their borders and settle within their lands. Ultimately the rich tapestry of the world will only ever be retained if different cultures maintain the traditions that define them. As such, different cultures can learn from and trade with each other, but should never live within each other's borders on a scale that alters the racial or cultural make-up of the host nation.

> **People are a product of the land they come from**
> **and should respect and honour that land.**

All peoples of the world have developed almost independently and often in vastly different environments. These different environments – nature itself – have moulded different people in different ways and given each race distinct characteristics. Not only should those characteristics be preserved and that diversity praised, but the environment that created those different races should be respected and honoured.

Despite the advancement of technology, Western man should not become a stranger to the land that shaped and moulded him and sheltered and provided for countless generations of his ancestors. Western man should reconnect with the natural world and strive to be as close to nature as possible and aim to live in harmony with the natural environment. To believe humanity is above nature is a dangerous fallacy – humanity still depends on the natural world and ultimately the natural world depends on humanity.

Western man should not pollute his lands nor should he treat his environment with disrespect or contempt. Western man should strive to show kindness to animals and compassion to those creatures that have less power than he – for nothing says more about a man than how he treats those less powerful than himself. Western man may be at the top of the food chain, but that does not give him the right to abuse that power or to inflict undue suffering upon the creatures that lie beneath him in that chain. The balance of the natural environment can be a delicate thing; it is best not to upset that balance, and man should strive to live as closely in harmony with nature as possible.

People should live in harmony with their natural environment and show kindness and respect to all living creatures.

A healthy and vibrant natural world and a connection with that world is food for the soul. Those who cut themselves off from nature and cocoon themselves in concrete separate themselves from their environment and disconnect themselves from the very world that gives them life. This leads to both a mentally and a physically unhealthy state – neither of which are conducive to a strong nation.

A nation's health lies in the health of its people – strong people build a strong nation.

A nation is only as healthy as the people who make up that nation. A nation full of slobs, drunkards and substance abusers will never be strong. A nation has the right to defend itself, but that nation must also have the ability to defend itself. A man can only defend his nation when he is strong and healthy. If Western man wishes to defend the soil that he calls home, then he must reject the poisons that ravage his body and strive for both physical and mental health.

Only through physical and mental health can individuals feel truly good about themselves. When people allow themselves to stagnate, they slip into a malaise which drags them down further and traps them in a negative cycle which spirals ever downward and carries them to self-defeat. Young and old alike should be encouraged to take up healthy pastimes in natural environments and embrace the natural highs that these pastimes provide.

All for one and one for all – stand together as a community.

Young and old should not just come together for pastimes; they should come together in every facet of life. Together we are strong, and divided we shall fall – Western man needs to rediscover the common bonds and cultural ties that once bound him to his brothers and sisters. Western man needs to re-awaken his desire for traditionalism and embrace the culture of his ancestors that has evolved over thousands of years.

Tradition and shared moral values are what bind a group of people; they are the glue that holds society together through the good times and the bad. Tradition is something that is passed down from generation to generation; tradition is what links the old to the new and connects the living with the dead. Tradition is the way that Western man not only shows reverence for the past; but in a very real way tradition allows Western man's ancestors to speak through him and express themselves long after they have left the mortal world.

Tradition and culture should be revered as they are the expression of the will of one's ancestors.

Once a people have lost their connection to their ancestors those people lose touch with their traditions. If you don't know where you have come from, how can you ever know where you are going, and if you don't know where you are going how can you know the purpose of your journey? Western man has been on a journey for thousands and thousands of years. Would it not be remiss of him to forget the details, the hardships, the achievements and the brave and noble sacrifices that were all part of that epic journey?

Tradition is expressed in many ways – through song, dance, dress, religious ceremony and literature. Those traditions should never be forgotten as they embody the mindset of generations past. To disconnect with one's ancestors and to fail to relate to, or even disrespect, the elders in a community, is to lose a vital connection that is central to the survival of a people. This spiritual bond with the past is something that can never be supplanted or replaced.

There is no higher goal in life than spiritual fulfilment – a fulfilment that flows from religion, folk, family and a connection with nature. Never must these spiritual callings be spurned in favour of the false idol of materialism. The pursuit of money and material wealth leads only to fleeting happiness. Attempting to fulfil the desire for material gain is a never-ending pursuit and leaves one feeling drained. To forgo spending time pursuing spiritual fulfilment in order to spend time chasing money is a grave error. Money and materialism should never come before family, folk, nature or religion.

Money is a tool of the economy and the economy exists to serve the people – not the other way around.

Western man would be wise to remember that money is only a medium of exchange and a barometer of material wealth – not a measure of spiritual fulfilment or happiness. True happiness and spiritual fulfilment are not fed and developed through buying ever more mass-produced and highly disposable products. In fact the pursuit of materialism brings depression and anxiety and weighs on one's soul. Materialism causes Western man to spurn his family, give up on having children and ultimately serves to enslave Western man through usury and debt.

Human beings value things they have struggled for and that they have worked hard to secure. Most importantly, it is through meaningful and genuine interactions with loved ones that lasting spiritual happiness and fulfilment can be attained. Instant gratification never lasts long, and the man who lives in a palatial but empty castle will ultimately feel less fulfilled than the man who lives in a modest abode but is surrounded by family and loved ones. Family and folk are truly the key to happiness and represent the very heart of Western society.

The traditional family is the cornerstone of Western society and should never be undermined.

The traditional family unit is the cornerstone of Western society and was born out of necessity and the will to survive. The family unit is the main reason why Western man is still here today, as the family unit underpins Western civilisation itself. This family unit has allowed Western man to become strong and has shaped not only the West, but the whole world. The foundation of any cohesive society and any community is the nuclear family – the hard-working father, the loving mother and the respectful and well-mannered children.

The nuclear family must be held up as the highest ideal, and defended at all costs. For it is within this nuclear family that every child develops the essence of what he or she will one day become. In every family unit the next generation learns from the previous generation. Parents set their children on a course – and it is imperative that the next generation continue on the correct path. Morality, values, discipline, order and traditions are passed down from father and mother to son and daughter.

The influence and importance of the family must never be underestimated. Much of what has been said earlier exposes a vicious and sustained attack on the family unit by the enemies of the West. To truly understand the importance of the family unit, one must only look at the lengths to which those who wish to see the West fall have gone in order to damage the traditional nuclear family.

Nationalism is the only ideology that embodies all of the tenets that have been listed above – but nationalism goes further and seeks to create and strive for what has been described as the perfect society. Through order, discipline and the creation of a homogenous society that thinks and operates with a shared consciousness, nationalism strives to create a better future for the community as a whole. Nationalism spurs the individual on to achieve more, but to achieve more for the greater good, not simply for selfish and materialistic reasons.

Nationalism is also the only political ideology that rejects both capitalism and communism. In a perfect society the economic system is based on productive enterprise. In a perfect society people are neither enslaved by materialism nor are they forced to work without incentive or reward. A society that embraces productive enterprise has both a social conscience to ensure that every level of society's hierarchy benefits from the success of industry, but also ensures that private ownership and profit are not removed from the economic equation.

So whilst individuals who own capital can profit from that capital, they do so not at the expense of their own workers, but by working with their employees in order to improve the means of production in a way that benefits everyone. In a capitalist society the owner of capital is not concerned with the rights or well-being of the worker; he is simply concerned with profit. Once the problems of capitalism manifest themselves within a society, the enemies of the West propose the false solution of communism. Communism seeks division by promoting class warfare in an unnatural drive for 'equality'. This class war targets those who own capital leading to a downward spiral in productivity as decision makers, inventors and owners are removed from the economic equation.

Make no mistake; both capitalism and communism are economic systems that are under the control of the enemies of the West. They are presented as two absolutes and as the sole alternatives to one another. But by creating this false dichotomy the enemies of the West have sought to ensure that no matter what option Western man chooses, he will always end up in the clutches of a system designed to defeat and enslave him.

Productive enterprise is a natural solution as it seeks to raise the standard of living for everyone and acknowledges that every level of society has a part to play in the advancement of that society. What's more, productive enterprise acknowledges that for society to advance successfully, it must move as one – for if it moves in separate directions it will tear itself apart. For if the worker moves in harmony with the business owner, both advance. For the worker and the business owner to move out of step with one another or for them to move in opposite directions would lead to tension, disharmony and ultimately create conflict within society.

Nationalism seeks to raise the standard of living for everyone in society – and although nationalism believes in structure and hierarchy, that structure and hierarchy is there for the benefit of all. Nationalism allows the best to rise to the top and seeks to promote excellence – and excellence is exactly what Western man needs right now.

Nationalism is the political and ideological embodiment of nature's will. Nationalism places the best in society on a pedestal in order to create role models and promote excellence. At the same time nationalism strives to create a homogenous society that pulls together in one direction and works toward common goals. Nationalism seeks to allow the best to rise to the top, but at the same time seeks to establish a safety net in order to ensure those who are less fortunate never fall onto the rocks of poverty. But above all else Nationalism seeks to enshrine the family unit, for that family unit is the core of a functioning and cohesive society.

Western man has slowly sunk in the abyss and embraced degeneracy, materialism and individualism. Western man has not only tolerated weakness and depravity, but has worshiped weakness and depravity as if they were virtues. Western man has truly lost his way, and in order to find it again he needs a beacon of hope to act as a light in a sea of darkness. The beacon of hope that Western man needs must embody awe-inspiring excellence – an excellence that will inspire Western man to rise again and be something better than he is now. But this excellence must not be wrapped up in selfish individualism; this excellence must instead embody the noble virtues of family, folk and soil, and seek to uphold Western culture, traditions and spirituality.

Like attracts like and good people follow good people. Equally, if a movement is dominated by losers, degenerates and weaklings it will only attract losers, degenerates and weaklings, and as a result will never achieve anything of note. The nationalists of past generations were writers, poets, artists, inventors, captains of industry, military geniuses, orators and athletes. That is what the West needs now – great men and women. The West needs great men and women to stand up and be counted. The West needs heroes to embrace a European revival that will shine like a beacon to Western man. The West needs brave men and women to stand up and inspire the masses. Large numbers of Western folk can now see the problems the West faces but are currently too scared to act – these people need leaders.

As Western man stands on the precipice and stares into the abyss, there are only two options: to embrace the fall and watch as Western civilisation crumbles, or to rise up and reclaim the West. Western man must either embrace a strong and righteous ideology that binds him to his community, or Western man will fall and all that has gone before will be forever lost.

There can be no half measures and there can be no room for cowards or individualistic and self-indulgent fools. There is no use in trying to play by the rules invented by the enemies of the West or by competing on a field that has been designed to ensure Western man loses every time. Those who seek to save the West must rise up and walk a difficult path, but a path that will inspire Western man and drag him back from the edge of defeat.

Walking this path may not be easy, and the journey may be long. Along this road one may encounter hardship and one may be forced to make difficult decisions. There may even come a time where great personal sacrifices must be made. But if you were to sacrifice yourself for a cause, could you find a more noble cause than the protection of your own folk and family?

25
REDEMPTION

Western man now stands on the very edge of the precipice and stares into the abyss. Western man faces extinction – both culturally and racially. This is not something that will happen in the distant future, but something that will happen within the next century; in fact Western man will find himself outbred and a minority in his own homelands within a matter of decades. Already the situation is critical with Western birth rates at an all-time low.

To see the reality of the demographic shift, one need only to look at the composition of primary schools in the Western world. In the UK nearly one third of primary school children are not ethnically British – and that is probably underestimating the extent of the problem. What's more, with huge numbers of immigrants entering Europe every month, the demographic trend will only accelerate over time and the situation for Western man will worsen.

But no matter how close Western man is to the edge, no matter how dark things may look and no matter how overwhelming the odds appear – there is always hope and there is always the chance for redemption. 'Only he is lost who gives himself up for lost' is an apt quotation and should never be forgotten. For as long as Western man has a will to fight and a will to survive he can seek redemption.

Western man must not stand with his head bowed and allow his spirit to be further weakened. Now is not the time for quiet contemplation or despair. Surely now is the time for the fightback to begin – for if a fightback does not happen now, then there will never be one. Western man must make a choice – he can either continue on his current path of individualism and hedonistic degeneracy, or he can rise again and reunite his blood, reclaim his soil and take charge of his own destiny. But rest assured; if he chooses the former he will face extinction.

However, for Western man to rise again, he must throw off the shackles that have been imposed upon him by the enemies of the West. The fightback starts with a change of mindset; Western man must first break the mental chains placed upon him and set himself free from the mental cage in which he has been imprisoned. This change of mind starts with each and every one of us. We must look at ourselves and assess how we have been affected by the ideological poison that has been fed to us. But in doing so we must be brutally honest and we must not fear admitting to the mistakes that we have made.

This book has exposed the way that Western man has been broken and the ways in which Western society has been undermined. This book has also exposed and critiqued many different vices and negative influences that Western man has embraced. The intention of this was not to insult or irritate – but to enlighten and educate. For despite some of the truths in this book being difficult to swallow, they are truths nonetheless.

It can often be hard to accept difficult truths – and even harder to accept truths that can appear as personal criticisms. But we have all made mistakes in our lives and not one of us is perfect. The ability to take criticism is the mark of a mentally developed and well-rounded adult. If one wishes to develop and mature, one must listen to criticism and act on it in order to strive to remove negative influences and behaviour from one's life.

The enemies of the West have had a great advantage when propagating the filth and degeneracy that they have pushed upon Western society. The vast majority of the poison that they pour out is not only extremely enjoyable, but it is also highly addictive. As such it would be impossible to find an individual that hasn't in some way bought into the debased material and degenerate lifestyles that are promoted by the enemies of the West.

You may have been promiscuous, you may have taken drugs, you may have spent weekends binge drinking, you may have embraced body modification or indulged in a lifestyle of overeating and laziness. The point is, at one time or another all of us have embraced vices, and all of us have been tainted by the degeneracy that surrounds us. As stated earlier, it would be impossible to live in a sewer and remain clean – and make no mistake; the West has become a moral sewer. We are all surrounded by so much poison and filth it would be impossible for it not to affect us in some way.

The important lesson is that we acknowledge the negative influences in our lives. We have all been tricked and misled by the divisive and anti-Western material that surrounds us, but once we are aware of the way we have been misled, it is important that we reassess where we are headed and change our direction in order to stop walking the wrong path. It takes great strength to admit to being fooled and to admit to having made mistakes and poor decisions. But only an imbecile or a pig-headed fool would continue down a road once it had been ably pointed out that they were headed to a dead end.

Before Western man can start thinking about saving his community, he must first look at himself and cast off the destructive influences that have affected him personally. All of us must do this, because if we are ever to start a clean slate, we cannot taint that clean slate with the poisonous influences that have brought the West to the brink. To start building a better future, Western man must separate himself from the poison that surrounds him. To start again with corrupting influences would only lead us back to where we are now.

Once we have freed ourselves from the influences that have destroyed the Western mind, poisoned the Western body, corrupted the Western soul and broken the Western heart can we set about building a new and better future, and we can set about putting Western man back on the right path. Once we have freed ourselves from the shackles placed upon us, we must rise up and strive for excellence in a way that would make our ancestors proud. We must embrace Western culture, traditionalism and rediscover the Western superego.

As individuals we must strive to be the best we can and base our vision of an ideal self on the idea of the Western superman. We must aim for excellence in everything we do and aim to be the ones that serve as an inspiration for others around us. We must become writers, artists, poets, athletes and captains of industry, and we must set an example for all so that when we come together as a community others look toward us as a beacon of everything that is good and strong.

Everyone has something they can excel at. It is important to try to be the best you can be and strive to make a difference. Attempt to make excellence part of your everyday life: be polite, be courteous, speak correctly, hold your head up high, present yourself in smart attire and be well groomed. Never allow yourself to get stuck in the pitfalls and traps laid out for you. Never settle for second best and most importantly never let yourself down and fail to give your all when it matters. For if you are content with failure and mediocrity you only play into the hands of those who wish to see Western man wiped from the face of the earth.

Once you have become the best you can be, join with others who share your goals and who also seek excellence. Work as a community, not just to better yourself, but to better everyone who is a part of that community. Once you have risen up and set an example, hold out your hand and help others who look toward you and wish to emulate what you have done. There is always someone worse off than you and someone who needs help; make it your duty to help that person rise so they can stand alongside you. This community spirit is what built the West and can serve to resurrect it even at this late hour.

By reconnecting with others around you, by building communities and by rediscovering what once bound Western man together, Western man can again be great. Make sure family and folk come first. Do not abandon your partner; do not turn your back on your brothers and sisters. Come together and treat your fellow man as you wish to be treated. Do not stop at simply building a community but go on to build a nation where you can be both safe and proud, a nation where you would want to bring up children, where the bonds between people are valued more highly than money and material objects. Discard the false idols of consumerism and materialism and build a society where happiness and fulfilment stems from spiritual pursuits.

But most importantly, find a partner who shares this outlook and wishes to stand by your side. Find a partner and do the most important thing you can do – bring children into this world and ensure that Western man is not a dying breed. Fill the schools and parks with the sound of Western children playing – and make sure your children are brought up in the ways that honour your ancestors. Make sure your children are healthy, polite and well-mannered and that they too set an example for others.

Build a lasting connection with one special person and bring children into this world – but also find a connection with the world itself and embrace nature. Reconnect with the land and soil that has provided for countless generations of Western man. Technology is fantastic and a testament to the inventive Western mind, but it should never be seen as an alternative to nature or serve to separate Western man from the natural world. Embrace a healthy lifestyle and teach your children to do the same.

Walk in the countryside, spend time in the natural world and take in the natural beauty of the West. Being around nature will make your soul bloom and give you a renewed vigour for life, making you strong and healthy on both a physical and mental level. Make sure you eat natural food and exercise regularly – free yourself from the poison that corrupts your body and has turned Western man from a warrior into an unwieldly slob.

Embrace the very things that were at the heart of the West and which allowed Western civilisation to grow and shape the world. Embrace family, folk and soil. As you do this, look back at the footsteps your ancestors left in the sand and honour the ways of the past – embrace traditionalism in all its forms and do not let the ways that have been alive for thousands of years perish and be forgotten. Our ancestors live on in our memories and in our actions; do not let them disappear and do not let their sacrifices be in vain.

Never forget that a small group of people can make a big difference – that a few dedicated men and women can inspire others and can change the course of history. From small acorns grow mighty oaks, and what might seem insignificant on a political and social level today, can one day change the whole world. Every great journey has a starting point and always begins when an individual or a group chooses to take those first steps. Take the first steps of your personal journey of improvement today – commit to fulfilling your potential and bettering yourself, not tomorrow, not next week, not in a month's time, but now.

The enemies of the West have a great advantage in that their poison is so addictive – but their poison also has a fatal weakness. The poison pushed upon Western man is intoxicating in the short term, but it always leaves those who embrace it feeling hollow and unsatisfied in the long term. This sense of dissatisfaction is experienced by so many Western folk, and is why so many suffer from depression and feel as if something is missing in their lives – these people are searching for something greater.

If a genuine, healthy and community-based alternative was placed in front of Western man, he would flock to it. People are attracted to strength, and gather around upstanding and strong individuals. By rising up and being the best you can be, you will yourself become a beacon of hope for the West. By coming together with other people like you and striving as a group to be even better, that beacon of hope will grow ever brighter.

Once Western man reconnects with the old ways and realises that spiritual fulfilment and the connection with blood and soil means more than the toxic poison being fed to him by the enemies of the West, he will once again be free. Once you have cast off the chains placed on your mind, you can help others do the same and work toward rebuilding our shattered communities. Once Western man has rediscovered his community and his culture, and once that community is again a strong and homogenous group, he can free his lands and take control of his own destiny once more.

Redemption for Western man is possible, but if that redemption is to come, it must come soon. The redemption of Western man starts with you. Rise, become the superman, walk tall in the footsteps of your ancestors, and rediscover what made Western man a titan and what made Western civilisation the towering accomplishment it once was.

The future is in your hands... Grasp it!

"Beyond doubt it would speedily verify the poverb that a nation must ravage itself before foreigners can ravage it, a man must despise himself before others can despise him."

Yukio Mishima, Runaway Horses